STRATEGIC GROWTH
FOR LEADERS

the For Leaders

SERIES

BOOK 2

Strategic Growth for Leaders

10 SUCCESS KEYS TO ELEVATE YOU TO THE NEXT LEVEL

Kelly Babcock, Ira Bowman, Carol Carpenter, Cynthia Davis,

Tom Finn, Dan Grech, River Jack, Liz Lathan, Dan Vega,

Megan McInnis, Nicole Osibodu & David Peters

EDITED BY **DEBORAH FROESE**

Library of Congress Control Number: 2024907450
ISBN: 978-1-954676-70-1 (hardcover)   978-1-954676-71-8 (ebook)

Although this publication is designed to provide accurate information about the subject matter, the publisher and the authors assume no responsibility for any errors, inaccuracies, omissions, or inconsistencies herein. This publication is intended as a resource; however, it is not intended as a replacement for direct and personalized professional services.

Editors: Marci Carson, Deborah Froese
Cover and Interior Design: Emma Elzinga

Printed in the United States of America

First Edition

3 West Garden Street, Ste. 718
Pensacola, FL 32502
www.indigoriverpublishing.com

Ordering Information:

Quantity sales: Special discounts are available on quantity purchases by corporations, associations, and others. For details, contact the publisher at the address above.

Orders by U.S. trade bookstores and wholesalers: Please contact the publisher at the address above.

With Indigo River Publishing, you can always expect great books, strong voices, and meaningful messages. Most importantly, you'll always find . . . *words worth reading.*

CONTENTS

INTRODUCTION

Henry **Ford had the right** idea when he said, "If everyone is moving forward together, then success takes care of itself." As a leader in your field, you'll identify with this notion. Undoubtedly, you have established approaches for putting teamwork into action.

But what is the measure of success?

Whether you're looking at starting a new business, achieving departmental goals, creating economic or environmental sustainability, or aiming for positive societal impact, success is quantified by growth. By more. Depending upon who you ask, more could relate to money, assets, staff, influence, products or services, or something else altogether. Growth, or attaining more—however you define it—is the subject of this second volume in Indigo River Publishing's *For Leaders* series.

As new technologies expand and converge, we are witnessing industry, connectivity, and innovation advance at accelerating rates. The emergence of generative artificial intelligence (AI) raises questions about the future of human agency. Add to that, the scale of global tension environmentally, economically, and politically—never mind residual effects of the COVID-19 pandemic—are upending the world as we know it. No matter how worthy the product or service you offer, approaching growth strategically is essential to keeping pace with change and extending your reach.

Consider *Strategic Growth for Leaders* to be an important tool to help navigate this new era. The contents explore methods of approaching change through deeper self-awareness; more finely-tuned business practices; building solid, authentic relationships with employees and clientele; and knowing when enough is enough.

Global growth is trending downward. According to Indermit Gill, the World Bank Group's Chief Economist and Senior Vice President:

> Without a major course correction, the 2020s will go down as a decade of wasted opportunity...Near-term growth will remain weak, leaving many developing countries—especially the poorest—stuck in a trap with paralyzing levels of debt and tenuous access to food for nearly one out of every three people. That would obstruct progress on many global priorities. Opportunities still exist to turn the tide. This report offers a clear way forward: it spells out the transformation that can be achieved if governments act now to accelerate investment and strengthen fiscal policy frameworks.[1]

In Gills's eyes, strong policy and financial frameworks initiated by governments open doors for growth and progress. While high-level policies are critical, individual leaders have the potential to create their own transformations, not only through financial considerations, but also through careful strategies and a sharper focus on other, more intrinsic aspects of themselves and their businesses.

Ayhan Kose, the World Bank's Deputy Chief to Indermit Gill and also the Director of the Prospects Group, points toward monetary policy and frameworks too. However, he also notes the importance of

---

1   "Global Economy Set for Weakest Half-Decade Performance in 30 Years," The World Bank, press release, January 9, 2024, https://www.worldbank.org/en/ news/press-release/2024/01/09/global-economic-prospects-january-2024-press-release#:~:text=Global%20growth%20is%20projected%20to,average%20of%20 the%20previous%20decade.

strengthening the "quality of institutions."[2]

Quantifying quality presents a challenge because it means different things to different people. Let's consider it in terms of human dignity, human welfare, and social justice. Progress for humankind. Simon Sinek addresses these concerns in his book, *The Infinite Game*. He contrasts the typical approach to business as a finite game resulting in winners and losers with the more altruistic notion of an infinite game bestowing benefit to all parties.[3] A finite game focuses on what can be won in the short term and thus creates aggressive competition. (Think quarterly results, which may prompt corner-cutting and disregard for social impacts in pursuit of growth.) In a finite game, trust and cooperation are replaced by fear.

On the other hand, an infinite game has longer-term objectives that may extend far beyond an individual's lifetime. (Consider the Indigenous perspective of seven generations; making decisions based upon future impacts.)[4] Playing an infinite game considers the well-being of everyone involved, from employees to customers, and even the environment. It draws upon strategies for vertical growth or increased impact rather than horizontal growth or multiplication of existing production or service capabilities, which often proves more costly.

The good news is vertical growth is powerful. In *The Infinite Game*, Sinek notes we achieve more by chasing dreams with a larger vision—that is, by playing the infinite game—than by racing against our competitors. Ultimately, playing the infinite game not only ensures a higher-quality institution, happier employees with a higher retention rate, and lasting client relationships, but results in greater financial gains.

---

2   Ibid.

3   Simon Sinek, *The Infinite Game* (New York: Portfolio/Penguin), 2019.

4   "What is the Seventh Generation Principle?" Indigenous Corporate Training, Inc., May 30, 2020, https://www.ictinc.ca/blog/seventh-generation-principle#:~:text=The%20Seventh%20Generation%20Principle%20is,seven%20generations%20into%20the%20future.

Shifting toward the infinite game makes sense. Consumers are looking for businesses who take creating a positive impact seriously. In an article published in late 2023, *Forbes* reports that "Socially responsible spending by consumers is going through the roof."[5] The article provides a few numbers to back up that statement. Of those surveyed:

- 71% felt it was important to support socially responsible brands.
- 66% said they had bought such products and services over the past year.
- 42% reported plans to spend more with socially responsible companies in 2024.

Strategic Growth for Leaders shares insights from successful leaders about understanding yourself, what you want to achieve, and ultimately, how to determine effective growth strategies for your business. Ten chapters, ten keys to success.

But there's more.

As we pulled this volume together, generative AI exploded on the scene with numerous apps and possibilities—everything from improved meeting note summation to writing copy and producing digital art—including photos representing real individuals in conjured situations. What does this mean for the future of creators? Of workers in general? Of honesty in media?

With reception ranging between excitement and fear, we thought it might be worth exploring what AI means for leaders and how one might determine effective use within their context for growth. We're happy to offer a bonus chapter demystifying this technology—which isn't as new as everyone seems to think it is.

According to bonus chapter contributor, River Jack, AI and

---

5   Amy Field, "Conscious Consumer Spending Could Be at A Tipping Point," Forbes, November 30, 2023, https://www.forbes.com/sites/annefield/2023/11/30/ conscious-consumer-spending-could-be-at-a-tipping-point/?sh=59f1621621ad.

humans are like teenagers. We've been around long enough to know something, but not everything, and we can't predict the implications of our behavior. "Teenagers, despite their unwavering sureness, and because of their developing pre-frontal cortex, can't comprehend what long-term consequences truly mean."

May *Strategic Growth for Leaders* prompt reflection, spark dreams, and provide inspiration for personal and corporate growth.

Deborah Froese
Executive Editor
Indigo River Publishing
March 7, 2024

CHAPTER 1

FIVE STEPS FOR GROWTH-MINDED LEADERSHIP

Kelly E. Babcock

Attorney, Management Consultant, Educator, Entrepreneur,
and Hemp Enthusiast/Cultivator

If you want to grow as a leader so that you can guide your team well, get ready to face new challenges. You may feel conflicted, unsure, or fearful and unworthy at times—yes, even as a leader. Change triggers deeply held limiting beliefs acquired through childhood or previous experiences and significantly impacts your ability to move forward. Moving past those challenges requires a leap of faith—faith in your plan, your partners, and your investors—but mostly, faith in yourself. To equip yourself to meet your leadership goals you'll need to cope with your limiting beliefs, accept who you are, and know who you want to become.

It's not easy, but it can be done. I'm living proof.

As a young person, I was a curious dreamer and an avid learner. Like many Gen Xers, I dreamed of going to college, scoring a good job, and saving for retirement. I did that. By the time I reached 30, I was a law school graduate and married with two kids, a house, and a dog. Gradually, and almost imperceptibly, I slid into survival mode on a double-income, double-kid household wheel of life. The hustle and bustle of daily routines became a numbing cycle. Options and opportunities that would have once energized my soul began to seem more like unrealistic dreams and missed chances.

I was stuck in survival mode.

Looking back, I see immobility had nothing to do with my situation, but it had everything to do with my mindset. I had accepted the idea that there wasn't enough time or money to dream, and therefore, my current state was my reality.

The human mind possesses an incredible ability to either limit or liberate an individual's potential. Many of my own limiting beliefs begin with the statement, "I can't," and probably originated in childhood. Growing up in rural Ohio, my ten-year-old-self viewed achieving a certain income level as evidence of success, so that's what my adult-self pursued. Since this was all done on the subconscious level and based on my core belief rather than an intentionally set goal, whenever I looked at opportunities exceeding that income level, my inner voice whispered, "You can't do that."

The idea of a growth mindset was popularized by psychologist Carol Dweck through her research into motivation and mindset and her best-selling book, *Mindset: The New Psychology of Success.*[1] A growth mindset refers to the belief that intelligence, abilities, and talents can be developed through dedication, effort, and continuous learning.

My own journey from desperation to freedom was not direct. It began with traditional therapy that probably saved my life but did nothing to let me feel as though I had any control over my destiny. The prospect of lifelong medication, mental health labels, and three-to-five Alcoholics Anonymous meetings a week were all reminders that, according to our healthcare system, I would never be "normal." After exhausting the few services my insurance covered, I felt compelled to seek a better way—and I found it.

---

1   Carol Dweck, *Mindset: The New Psychology of Success* (New York, NY, Random House, 2006).

Dan Harris's 2014 bestseller, *10% Happier*,[2] and other quality books like the one you are reading now, podcasts, and free online courses led the way. As I navigated feelings of unworthiness, self-doubt, and fear, I came to realize that my mind created the uneasiness I felt and the way I viewed the world. Exploring the science of the mind and how thoughts and feelings create behavior reignited my innate curiosity. Luckily, I found mentors who helped me look at my thoughts objectively and retrain my brain.

All these supports helped remove the imaginary limitations I had put in place over the years to support an illusion of safety, the ideas that kept me playing small. How could I grow or dream or lead a team that way? As I began to evaluate my core beliefs, I recognized where childhood experiences related to money, time, relationships, and spirituality had created limiting beliefs, and that kick-started a mental transformation, which allowed me to grow personally and professionally. I could finally open myself to new experiences and opportunities.

If you want to grow, your mind has to be in the right place. With some dedication and effort, you can achieve a growth mindset through five steps: Intention, Confidence, Action, Influence, and Impact.

Step 1: Intention

What do you want to do? What do you want to achieve? Establishing your intention is the first step toward achieving a growth mindset. Clarity of purpose provides direction and motivation. Keeping your intention at the forefront of all your activities keeps them on track.

Setting an intention that you truly believe in, one you can encourage your team to support too, involves identifying specific goals, dreams, or aspirations, and shaping a plan to achieve them. It takes a lot of self-reflection and soul-searching. This is also a continuous process. If

---

2   Dan Harris, *10% Happier: How I Tamed the Voice in My Head, Reduced Stress Without Losing My Edge, and Found Self-Help That Actually Works—A True Story* (It Books, 2014).

you're uncertain about what you want to do, setting an intention can be scary. Fear tends to prompt procrastination or indecision. So, shove those worries aside and focus on what you want rather than what you don't want. Begin by paying attention to your patterns of thinking. If your plans depend upon avoiding certain outcomes, look for the limiting beliefs fencing you in.

If you are starting a new business or seeking growth in an existing one, now is the time to objectively evaluate your core beliefs and values. What do you believe about life and limitations? What do you most value? Identify any areas where you question your self-worth or abilities and acknowledge areas where you have already achieved your goals to remind yourself what you're capable of.

Challenge and dismantle those limiting beliefs. Ask yourself *why?* a lot. Remember, nothing is impossible unless you tell yourself it is. Through introspection and self-awareness, identify the deep-rooted beliefs that create resistance or obstacles to your growth.

A big hurdle for many people is money. Where I grew up, it wasn't uncommon to distrust people with a lot of money. What is your relationship with or attitude toward money and your own value in the marketplace? Deep down, do you think you have to be ruthless to be rich, or that only winners are wealthy?

Any hidden limiting beliefs that conflict with your intention will stop you cold. Even if one part of you knows you have the potential to achieve your goals, the persistent negative self-talk of misaligned core beliefs creates self-doubt. When external achievements exceed your sense of worthiness, you may downplay your contribution to success by claiming you were just lucky or in the right place at the right time.

If you're not consciously aware of any internal "dis-ease," conflict can spark a search for what's "missing" in life—the next big thing, the next job, the next city. Inner conflict can even cause self-sabotage, keeping you stuck in scarcity thinking (a belief that resources are limited), procrastination, and perfectionism. Over time, that kind of misalignment has the potential to create serious negative consequences in your personal life, your business, and your professional relationships.

Setting clear intentions and engaging the appropriate belief structure to achieve them makes it possible to reawaken or even create a new growth-oriented mindset.

Step 2: Confidence

How do you see yourself? Are you confident, or do you suffer from a persistent feeling of inadequacy and self-doubt despite evidence of competence and success? This condition, known as *impostor syndrome*, plagues many people, even high-achievers. It hinders progress. It can lead individuals to undermine their own accomplishments and hold them back from embracing opportunities or taking authentic action.

The way you look at yourself is shaped by your core beliefs, the ideas and perspectives that were passed on to you by early childhood caregivers. Even if you are aware of such beliefs, it's not easy to step around them. As you test new and more empowering ideas, challenge past fears, and seize opportunity, you will likely feel uneasy or unsure—like a baby giraffe on roller skates. Because change creates dissonance between old and new, periods of transformation can make you feel like an impostor in both worlds—the world you are in and the one you want to create.

Embracing a growth mindset stretches you beyond what you have achieved thus far, and it instills confidence. Start shifting your perspective by recognizing any self-talk that pulls you into old, negative patterns of behavior. Replace those negative thoughts with positive ones. Push past imposter syndrome by recognizing each accomplishment, no matter how small, as confirmation that you are achieving your goals. By stepping outside of your comfort zone, you'll see what you're really capable of. Then, watch, fear transform into excitement, conviction for your purpose, and confidence.

Psychology and neuroscience provide a plethora of research explaining how it is possible to change the way we think, which in turn will change what we believe about our abilities and potential. One of my favorite quotes comes from the late Dr. Wayne Dyer: "Change the way you look at things, and the things you look at change."

Believe that you are already successful and allow yourself to feel the feeling of success. When you change your perspective about who you really are, you will turn feelings of inadequacy and self-doubt into excitement and empower yourself to empower your team.

Step 3: Action

Growth is not passive. It requires action. Many people get stuck in the planning phase of goal-setting, never making the moves required to bring their aspirations to life. Take that first step, no matter how small or how uncomfortable it is. It's pivotal for growth. Stepping outside of your comfort zone builds the confidence I mentioned earlier, and it also creates momentum. Even if the results are not what you expected, you took action and learned something.

If you are planning to start a new business, file your LLC, create a business plan or pitch deck, or find a mentor, just do SOMETHING. Move intention into existence. Small actions produce some results. Larger, higher-risk actions have potential for bigger outcomes. In the beginning, it isn't necessarily the size of the action or the outcome that makes the most difference; rather, it is the process of initiating and following through, which creates a feeling of accomplishment and nurtures a positive mindset.

Those who fall into the perfectionism trap are most prone to getting stuck in the planning stage. Even high-performing leaders mistake effort for accomplishment. This can frustrate a growth-oriented leader!

Constantly overanalyzing, second-guessing, and looking for confirmation or validation suggest core beliefs are still misaligned. Reduce the internal conflict, and new, creative ideas will begin to flow. More is accomplished with your time. So, initiate action steps to capitalize on any opportunities that are in alignment with your intentions and core beliefs. You'll find work and decision-making becoming effortless and action flows with greater ease.

Step 4: Influence

As you open your mind to new experiences along your growth journey, you will accumulate valuable knowledge, experiences, and insights. To gain influence, communicate your newfound wisdom to others. Influencing and inspiring others not only reinforces your growth mindset but also creates a positive ripple effect in personal and professional circles. In your personal life and in areas where you have influence, modeling the principles of growth through positive thinking and consistent positive action toward team members, family and friends will put you on the path to growth.

As you evaluate and eliminate old patterns and beliefs, try to identify where those limiting beliefs originated. As mentioned previously, they may represent childhood programming. In some cases, they may have been instilled from a corporate policy, culture, or leadership perspective. If your role allows you to make changes within these structures and systems, use your new knowledge to influence those practices. Share your intentions and beliefs with your partners, team leaders, and staff.

If you are not the person responsible for effecting changes to organizational norms, you may have some power to influence them. Growth-minded leaders are not threatened by new and innovative ideas. They understand that "you don't know what you don't know," and they're open to hearing your thoughts. However, those with limited or fixed mindsets may feel threatened. Put yourself in their shoes. Understand their point of view, the source of any fears and limiting beliefs, and anticipate what they will want from you to support the changes you would like to see.

When working with a fixed-mindset leader, you may have to communicate through old patterns of thinking to effectively influence them. Remember, each person is on their own journey. Pointing out that you are aware of something that they have not yet conceived of could feel threatening. Know your audience, be mindful of your language and tone, and most of all, be patient with those who are not yet as aware as you are.

Mentoring, coaching, or actively engaging in knowledge-sharing platforms fosters a sense of accountability and reinforces the belief in continuous learning. Moreover, through influencing others, individuals reinforce their understanding of concepts and develop a deeper mastery of their own skills.

Step 5: Impact

The final step for growth-minded leadership is to expand your circle of influence and make a far-reaching difference in the lives of others. It is the culmination of your intentions, beliefs, actions, and influence.

From a personal growth perspective, impact appears through improved relationships, increased emotional intelligence, and a greater sense of fulfillment and happiness. On a business or societal vector, impact manifests in various forms, from improved performance in business ventures to enhanced creativity and innovative problem-solving abilities.

Don't downplay your accomplishments; record your achievements and any positive feedback received. It's evidence of your competence, progress, and impact. Seize every opportunity to celebrate the positive impact you create, small and large. Each result leads you closer to fulfilling the goals, dreams, and aspirations you set out to attain.

~

Embracing a growth mindset is key for effective leadership. Take the five steps outlined here by setting a clear intention, building confidence, taking action, influencing others, and ultimately, you'll create a lasting impact. You'll not only overcome self-imposed limitations, but you'll also inspire others to do the same, creating a positive and enduring impact on society as a whole.

CHAPTER 2

FIND YOUR DRIVING FORCE

Carol Carpenter

Founder, MotoVixens LLC/CC Track Events; Managing Partner,
Iron Dog Media; Founder, Selenion Strategy Group

I **began my journey toward** leadership when I was a young Taiwanese
woman burdened by the duties and responsibilities of my culture,
studying to become a doctor, losing my mother to cancer, and re-eval-
uating my life. Ultimately, I ended up doing what I never imagined I
would do: divorcing. Overcoming those situations to discover my passion—my driving force—led to an incredible array of experiences. They
taught me how to rise above my circumstances, embrace everything
life has to offer, and find my true purpose through entrepreneurship.

When I started my first business, MotoVixens, I was in the midst
of a divorce. It was a double-edged sword. On one hand, it marked
an end to 21 years of marriage and raising children, and on the
other, it signaled the beginning of a new chapter in my life, one that
included motorcycles.

Who would have ever thought?

When we married, my husband and I had agreed that I would be
a stay-at-home mom, something I am grateful I had the opportunity

to do. However, it meant leaving the workforce for two decades. The valuable skills and knowledge I once had in the medical and financial industries became obsolete. And I wasn't young anymore.

Suddenly, I was *that* woman: divorced and in her early 40s.

Much to everyone's surprise, I didn't go out and find a job immediately. Instead, I started doing things I had never had the chance to do before by going through my bucket list, which included learning to ride a motorcycle. Naturally, everyone around me thought I was experiencing a midlife crisis. Looking back now, that moment marks the time I actually regained control of my own life and my sense of self. Like so many other women, I had spent my entire life taking care of others and putting my own needs aside, believing it was my duty, obligation, and responsibility. My culture dictated right from birth my role in the family, and even though I was born in the U.S., those commitments, unwritten and yet binding, were powerful.

I never planned to become an entrepreneur, but as soon as I discovered my passion for motorcycles, signs and opportunities appeared everywhere—and I was listening. I got into motorcycling at a time when it was still uncommon to see women on motorcycles unless they were passengers. As a result, I struggled with issues like being able to find the appropriately styled and sized gear and understanding how to modify my motorcycle without giving up performance. Because women are minorities in the motorcycle industry, we were mostly disregarded. Issues like these were an entry barrier for many. I quickly recognized an opportunity: if more women were to ride, these issues needed to be addressed. Who better than another woman to do so?

I took it a step further and started racing, determined to obtain my expert racing license. I wanted to prove to myself and other women that it is never too late to chase a dream. The desire to become an expert at my craft fueled my passion for the sport. I started instructing, and a few short years later, pivoted to start an educational motorcycle organization.

In 2012, I launched MotoVixens to help train women riders and create a community among them. That has now become even more inclusive. We welcome riders of all genders and backgrounds, and riders of all styles of motorcycles—from dirt to adventure to cruisers and Harleys. Now, here we are, more than 12 years later, and MotoVixens is the only woman-owned track day organization in the Pacific Northwest—and the one with the highest safety rating.

Embrace Risk

Starting MotoVixens was one of the hardest things I'd ever done. I had never started a business before and had no idea of how to do it. On top of that, no one had ever challenged the status quo in this male-dominated industry. However, I believed so strongly in my cause that I put everything on the line financially to see it to fruition. It never occurred to me that I would be met with so much resistance that I would eventually wonder if it was worth it to continue.

I saw it as a risk—and it's human nature to avoid risks, right?

But is it really? Who put this limiting idea in my head? In yours?

It doesn't belong.

From the day we are born, we are hardwired to take risks in order to survive. If we didn't, we would all remain in diapers, dependent on someone else, and unable to speak or move around. The ability and willingness to take risks is ingrained in us. It's how we learn and evolve. Babies want to discover the world around them. They innately roll over one day to discover they can crawl. Then, as their muscles strengthen, they start to walk, allowing them to satiate their curiosity about the world around them. There is no fear involved, no inner chatter warning them it can't be done.

So, then, what causes us to see something as natural as growth and expansion as a risk?

I'm reminded of a conversation with a friend about a helicopter parent, a dad who hovered around his son, never letting the boy make mistakes or get hurt. When problems arose, instead of allowing his son to consider possible solutions, Dad came to the rescue. But standing in front of your children like a shield at every turn causes harm in the long run. It conditions them to see risk as something negative, something to be fearful of, rather than an opportunity to learn from mistakes, solve problems on their own, or gain the confidence and skills necessary to meet life's inevitable challenges.

It may seem counterintuitive, but learning to take risks gives us more control. As we test and survive new experiences, we build the confidence needed to strategize and take larger risks. Lowering risk aversion helps us view our circumstances from a different perspective. It widens our comfort zone and provides the security we've been seeking all along.

Strategic risk-taking fuels growth for us and for our businesses.

The biggest wall between humans and risk-taking is the fear of failure, however, failure isn't negative. Failure provides valuable data that helps determine what did and didn't work so we can make the necessary adjustments and try again, refining until you succeed. Failure can only come if you are doing something, so rather than wear that as a badge of shame, it should be a badge of honor.

Know Your Why

Finding something that you are deeply passionate about and drives you, with a purpose larger than monetary gain, can lead to remarkable outcomes. This is your *why*. My *why* has always been about helping and elevating others. The joy I get from participating in someone else's success, their moments of elation and epiphany, is unlike anything else. It is pure and utter excitement, the kind that can't be adequately articulated, just *felt*. It resonates through mind, body, and soul.

When you find a business idea that deeply resonates with you, first make sure engaging with it keeps your *why* intact. Why do you do what you do? Your *why* is really your purpose. Your purpose will drive you every single day, shape a vision or long-term aspirations for your business, and inspire others.

I reflect on my *why* every day, especially when things get tough. I play a recorded "mind movie" once in the morning and once in the evening. It's a collection of affirmations, motivational sayings, and images accompanied by music. The lyrics and visuals have deep personal meaning. They remind me of my *why*. Keeping my purpose out front reminds me of the impact I want to make, and that helps me focus on my vision, or my goal.

Once you've discovered your *why*, you'll need to establish a vision to achieve it.

When I started MotoVixens and the other companies that followed (Iron Dog Media and Selenion Strategy Group), I had a concrete *why* but I didn't have a clear vision or the *how*—the strategies, methods, and actions that would help achieve my *why*. I trusted that as I moved forward, the *how* would reveal itself. It always does. Do the work, work hard, move forward, and when the time is right, the path reveals itself.

Over time, everything changes—economically, politically, socially, and so on—and any of those changes have the potential to impact your business both positively and negatively. Having a vision—a long-term goal—and holding fast to it avoids confusion and, quite possibly, failure. It allows you to shift gears when you need to but allows you to keep heading in the same direction. The end goal, no matter how lofty or impossible it may seem, *is* possible, as long as your vision remains strong and absolute.

Share Your Why

You can't be successful alone. You need a team. To achieve your goals, share your vision with your team. Be clear about everyone's responsibility to work collectively. I have weekly meetings with my core team and advisors to ensure each of my companies keeps moving toward its goals. Without these meetings, focus is lost. We can't move forward collectively without the same goal in mind.

My vision isn't necessarily specific to any one company or industry. It stems from what I am passionate about and where I can see a need. Many times, it is about empowering and inspiring women, but I don't want to do it with words alone. I want to lead by example. If I haven't walked the walk, how can I possibly speak about the subject with honesty and integrity?

That realization made me decide to race. If I wanted to inspire other racers, I had to understand every aspect of what it took to be on the track. Only then could I truly help and be empathetic to their challenges and experiences.

When I see a need that captures my interest, I look for platforms where I can elevate it, such as writing articles or books, creating a podcast or appearing as a guest on one, or finding opportunities for public speaking—such as my TEDx talk on risk.[1] Then I seek ways to create a large and lasting positive impact by finding the right audience for the subject matter and medium.

If my vision can satisfy passion, need, platform, and impact, I'm 100% in!

When your *why* is about the greater good and creating a large impact, it takes on a life of its own, and pretty soon you realize that instead of driving it, it drives you, and you want to share it.

MotoVixens started with a plan to provide women motorcycle riders with a supportive community. It meshed with my desire to help others, create opportunity, and make the largest possible positive impact in the motorcycle industry. Inclusion resulted—and not just inclusion of women. Men also wanted to join the supportive culture we were creating. MotoVixens became about riders—all riders.

---

1   Carol Carpenter, "Can Risk Give You Security?" filmed October 2022 at TEDx Wilmington, Wilmington, DE, video, 10:47, https://www.youtube.com/watch?v=O7MLtCgUUaQ.

When my journey began, I believed everyone could see where the industry was going. "Women are the future of this sport," I would tell anyone who would listen.

I didn't speak out of arrogance—it was more of a prediction—but I felt very strongly about it. I didn't stop to evaluate the impact of my words or to acknowledge that because I often see things from a different perspective than most. It never occurred to me others might not understand. I was laughed at and told there weren't enough women in our sport to make any difference. The naysayers were unable to see what I saw. I *knew* women would inspire future generations, encouraging and mentoring young riders and females to believe they can achieve whatever they put their minds to.

I often wish I had a video of me proclaiming this prediction to remind myself, when I am struggling, that what I said so long ago is indeed coming true! If I've learned anything it is this: follow your intuition, it will not lead you astray.

Overcome Obstacles

In the early days, trying to create a women-run track organization came with extraordinary challenges. Motorcycling is a male-dominated industry. The boys' club culture is real. Their relationships with one another span decades, and they collaborate behind the scenes to keep any competition at bay—or even annihilate them. The boys' club did not want to share their territory with newcomers—especially a woman. No one challenged their way of doing things until I came along. The old adage came into play: everyone wants you to get ahead, they just don't want you to get ahead of them.

At the time, I wasn't interested in being a full-fledged track day organization. I organized a couple of "one-off" days at the track and worked as an instructor at several organizations. As one of just a few females promoting our sport, I provided value to each of those organizations.

Nothing changed until they began to see me as a threat.

I operated outside the box. I used social media videos as marketing tools and offered promotions and sponsorships. When I began drawing attention, one organization emailed me to say my service was no longer required. When I emailed back to ask why, I was told I "had an agenda."

I responded with a request for a call to explain, but I was not granted one. That stung. After spending several years helping them make money—with no financial gain for myself—I was discarded and then ignored. Within a few weeks, another organization I worked for texted me a similar message.

Those messages were like a punch to the gut. These were people whom I had thought were my friends. As long as I was nothing more than a bubbly girl promoting the sport by marketing their company and products, helping them make money, I was useful. Once they viewed me as a threat, they took the opportunity to ban me collectively.

Little did they know I would not leave quietly. However, it took all my courage just to hang on.

Courage draws upon your ability to stay the course, innovate, and overcome the most difficult of times. Courage means taking situations that might cripple others and finding a silver lining, even if it's only a sliver, while continuing to inspire others, always maintaining a positive perspective. It means listening rather than reacting to criticism sent your way, because in that criticism, you'll find what your opponents are fearful of. It is not about you; it's about their shortcomings. Once you spot those shortcomings, you can strategize the best defense and hopefully, in the end, be victorious.

Courage often leads to taking the road less traveled, becoming a maverick within your industry, and making change to create more opportunities. The road can be lonely at times, and others may not understand or share your excitement about your accomplishments. You may even encounter resistance and question if it's worth continuing. Understanding your *why* will keep you focused on your goal and fuel your courage—no matter what.

Discovering I no longer had a place to ride or share my love of the sport with others crushed me. People I had instructed side by side with wouldn't speak up for me, shunning me instead. But the situation was bigger than me. It was a David and Goliath story, and I was faced with a challenge that would require all the aforementioned attributes of courage—and an even bigger dose of tenacity. My passion for this sport and what I believed I could bring to it drove me to continue onward.

I did what they didn't think I could do; I became their competition.

I chose to navigate shark-infested waters with the sole purpose of helping the sport I loved. Diving in refueled my sense of purpose. By drawing more women to the sport, inspiring, encouraging, and mentoring them, I took back the control they thought they had stripped away from me.

That was what drove me then, and it continues to drive me now. Every day.

Adjust and Persevere

While your vision should remain fixed, your *how*—or your strategy for achieving it—can vary. Strategy allows room to think outside of the box and make necessary changes to survive. It becomes a "have to" mentality instead of a "need to" state of mind. When you *have* to do something, it happens right away, forcing you to move forward, and possibly allowing room for innovation and accelerated growth. When you *need* to do something, you are more inclined to think about all the reasons not to do it and never get around to doing it at all.

Think of strategy as the road to your destination. Your destination could be someplace like Newport Beach, California. Depending on where you begin, and the places you wish to explore, there are many ways to plot your route. The route you choose impacts travel time. So do unexpected weather and road conditions that may force you to adjust your route—or even giving in to a tempting scenic detour. So it is with planning your strategy to accomplish your vision. Strategy allows you to adjust or refine the route to your goal as needed, as unexpected circumstances arise along the way.

We saw keen evidence of this during the COVID-19 pandemic. It significantly changed the speed with which we did business and even halted many businesses for a period in time. Those who could, pivoted as they waited for conditions to return to some form of normalcy. Others played the waiting game while hoping to resume business as usual. Many others had to fold.

In the early years of MotoVixens, overcoming adversity while dealing with the boys' club was incredibly frustrating. They controlled the rules of the game and kept changing the goal posts, forcing me to change my strategies constantly. After spending several years slowly gaining ground, I would come close to the finish line without managing to cross it—because they kept moving it!

At one point, a continuous sense of failure almost caused me to throw in the towel. It was my style to avoid confrontation and keep moving forward, but that was becoming increasingly harder to do. They kept forcing my hand, and things got ugly. Affiliations between various organizations and individuals prevented me from reserving time at specific tracks. My competitors threatened my staff and attacked me publicly on social media about unrelated events. They vilified and slandered me and what I stood for. They had my social media accounts pulled. People with industry influence were spreading lies, knowing that others would blindly believe them.

To make matters worse, defending myself against rumors would make me look guilty—but so would *not* defending myself.

I couldn't win.

My advisors told me the slanderous behavior spoke volumes about my competition: they were afraid of me! That meant I was a threat to them. With that epiphany, my perspective changed, and I began to look at their continued attacks as a compliment. It gave me the little push I needed. I found the strength to continue and focus on my *why*.

My *why* was worth the effort. I had fought too long and hard, and I could not—*would* not—quit. I would not allow my competitors to win and continue bullying others. What message would quitting relay to all the women I represented?

If I was going to lead by example, then it was up to me to continue fighting for what was fair and right.

How hungry are you? How badly do you want to accomplish your goal? Does your *why* fuel you to continue even when everything in your being wants to quit? Do you have it in you to persevere through the most difficult of situations?

Even if you are courageous enough to take the first step toward bringing your idea to life through vision and strategy, without perseverance it will fall apart.

Perseverance is both a habit and a mindset. It's about being able to continue working even when you are tired and want to quit. It's about ignoring the pain, being so laser-focused on your goal that pain is relegated to the background.

Fuel Your Passion

As an entrepreneur, passion for what you do creates a high threshold for pain and discomfort. Passion gives you the power to overcome any and all obstacles. Your level of passion directly correlates with your physical energy and your ability to stay the course.

Passion is necessary for both your professional and personal life. If you only focus on work, you aren't honoring the whole you. Find activities that light you up outside of work. Whether it is golf, fishing, cooking, traveling—or even motorcycling—it's about nurturing every aspect of you to take care of you. If you aren't at your best, how can you possibly have the drive or focus to reach your goals?

Don't confuse the time you take to better yourself with selfishness. Self-care is not a luxury; it's fuel for the drive. The level at which your passion burns is the secret to your level of enthusiasm and perseverance. Devour knowledge with insatiable hunger; exercise your mind, body, and soul regularly; and take pride in how you care for yourself, because how you present yourself to the world is how the world will treat you.

Being disciplined about self-care is just as important as being disciplined about achieving your goals. Self-care ties into self-worth. If you don't have time to take care of yourself, then you are showing others you aren't worth much. If you want others to value you, you first have to value yourself. You are your most valuable asset, without a fully-rounded you, your aspirations will never be realized.

Find Support

We are humans. Over lengthy periods of difficulty, we wonder if the struggle is worth it. Negative inner chatter creeps in and we start to doubt ourselves. That's normal; it happens to the best of us. How we choose to respond is what will ultimately play a role in the outcome. Can you take hardship and use it positively? Can you spin it into something that helps you to move forward? The proper mindset and perspective can help tremendously with perseverance.

Support a healthy perspective by surrounding yourself with like-minded individuals who have also navigated choppy waters successfully, people who want to see others succeed, can see opportunity instead of obstacles, and offer sage advice.

The people you surround yourself with greatly influence how you view the world. If you surround yourself with people who project limited beliefs, those limited views impact your decisions and reduce your ability to resist hardships and challenges. Surround yourself with optimistic, successful individuals, movers and shakers, mavericks, and most of all, people with integrity and strong core values. Gain knowledge and learn to view the world from their perspective. The lens they view the world through is not the cloudy lens most of us grew up with. Once you've had the chance to view the world through a clearer lens, you'll realize you have more control over your destiny than you originally thought you did.

Drive Opportunity

MotoVixens was launched in 2012. Twelve years is a long time for any company, never mind an industry that has taken a beating financially since 2008. Despite industry conditions, I had the joy of building a company based on my passion and turning it into a platform for all riders. I continue to find new ways to elevate and market the industry to ensure its survival and continuous growth.

When you have the opportunity to be a part of something larger than yourself—with a mission, vision, and goal that serves a larger purpose—magical things happen. Opportunities I never could have imagined resulted from my efforts: a signature series product line, a reality show, a podcast, partnership in Iron Dog Media, starting Selenion Strategy Group, becoming executive producer for an upcoming film, writing several magazine articles, giving a TEDx talk, becoming a comic book character inspired by my story, and publishing an Amazon best-seller, *The Elegant Disruptor.*[2] I've had the incredible opportunity to partner with or invest in ventures with positive global impact, including Amani Resorts, The Business Ethics and Education Commission (BEEC), and Azure Printed Homes.

We do not get to choose how we enter the world, nor do we get to choose how we leave it. Life is full of uncertainty. Nothing is guaranteed. It becomes what we choose to make of it. I get out of bed every morning knowing that I want to leave this world a better place and impact many people in a positive way, and I do that one step at a time.

What drives you?

---

2   Carol Carpenter, *The Elegant Disruptor,* independently published, 2022. https://a.co/d/dPD5PDE.

CHAPTER 3

INCREMENTAL MONUMENTAL CHANGE

Cynthia Davis

Trusted Disruptor; Executive Mentor and Author; Partner, Radiant Blue, LLC; Founder, Incremental Monumental Change Leadership

> *Success is the progressive realization of a worthy ideal.*
> — Earl Nightingale in *The Strangest Secret*

Is it possible to live day by day, moment by moment, knowing that you are moving consistently toward your goal with every decision you make? Is it possible to generate extraordinary results, achieve extraordinary success, and have a deep sense of fulfillment and purpose along the way?

If you think not, I hope to challenge your thinking with an alternative view. If you think the idea might be possible but don't know how others have managed to break from conventional methods of getting results, I'm here to help. Let me share what I have learned from others who consistently enjoy ever-expanding experiences of impact, growth, and personal fulfillment through incremental monumental change (IMC).[1]

---

1   Incremental Monumental Change is Cynthia Davis's approach to leadership and growth. https://incrementalmonumentalchange.com/.

You Have the Power to Create Success

Years ago, I adopted a definition of success based upon the Earl Nightingale quote introducing this chapter. My version: success is the continued momentum toward *your* worthy goal. That's right, YOUR worthy goal. It's unique and personal, and if it is on your heart to experience that goal, then the wherewithal to achieve it is embedded within your desire.

Wow! That's a pretty bold statement.

Let's break it down.

The vast majority of people believe life is happening *to* them. A few believe that life is happening *for* them. But here's the thing: whether you believe that life is happening *to* you, or life is happening *for* you, you're accepting the belief that external factors are more in control of your life than you are. Yet, in this very moment, you are living with the cumulative effects of a series of day-by-day, moment-by-moment choices and decisions that *you* made.

Those who express leadership through the lens of IMC have learned that they have the power to create life experiences instead of simply responding to external factors. This is the concept often associated with Gandhi: "Be the change you want to see in the world."

The success train can't leave the station with the belief that "life is happening to me" fueling its engines, and it certainly can't gain full momentum with the slightly improved belief that "life is happening for me." However, knowing "I AM the change I want to experience in the world" throttles the success train to gain momentum for full speed ahead.

A New Form of Leadership

What would it be like to set the course to your goal and know with certainty that you will achieve that goal, that you are making the wisest choices day by day, moment by moment in its direction? What would it be like to choose and generate your future vision, create your monumental impact, and achieve your audacious goals?

With speed, clarity, and confidence every step of the way, IMC leaders do that and more. They know the best way to predict the future is to create it, and they know the wisdom it takes to create the future is found internally. They use their deep desire or dream and the "code" imprinted on it as a guide, leading them step by step, moment by moment, day by day, to make the wisest choice in the direction of their goals.

In doing what I love and what inspires me, I traveled the path of a corporate executive as the CEO of a publicly traded company; authored a best-selling book;[2] built a tribe of wisdom warriors; created the mastermind immersive program, "Leaders of Distinction"; and designed the executive and entrepreneurial transformational experience, "Transcending Business as Usual." Each of these accomplishments taught me how to predict the future by creating it.

So, while you may find that concept interesting and philosophically agree with me, the question becomes, *how is that possible?* How do I learn to lead others and live without struggle, sleepless nights, indecision, and fear?

After years of adhering to business protocols of serious strategic planning, collecting reems of data, engaging in discussions and debates, and employing analytics and competitive analysis, I have concluded that the typical approach to growth is a self-perpetuating and very expensive illusion. Despite all the strategic planning, meetings, and studies, business would usually continue in its current form: status quo. Perhaps here and there a new contract might be won, a new customer found, or a slight shift in market share achieved. However, I suspect that if I were to evaluate what it actually cost in people, time, and resources to achieve those gains, the victory would be somewhat hollow.

---

2   Cynthia Davis and Rachel Hetzel, *In Search of Wisdom: Six Master Keys to Living the Life You Want and Deserve*, Black Card Books Division of Gerry Robert Enterprises, 2016.

So, let's shift the way we look at growth. Let's explore how market disruptors, innovators, extreme pioneers, mavericks, and "playing full out" entrepreneurs, think differently. They certainly do not spend most of their time looking through the rear-view mirror to compare trends of performance of this month with the same month last year. And they are certainly not spending eons of time strategizing about what may or may not happen in the future—as if all the planning in the world could predict it. Too much bureaucracy and endless questioning with slow to no decision-making processes sucks people dry. Who has time for this? It's a real loss of talent when possibility thinkers and mavericks are sidelined until they can't take it anymore and leave.

I know many people who left the corporate world and went on to lead successful startup companies where their creativity was not squelched by corporate stagnation. We need a world of entrepreneurs and business leaders who have the capability and willingness to use their ideas, vision, and passion to lead growth, advancements, and innovations, creating good within themselves, their businesses, and even humanity. These leaders take the world to the next level, and that's what IMC is all about.

Throughout my career, I have had the opportunity to work with numerous business leaders and entrepreneurs. I made it my life's work to understand what separated the wheat from the chaff. You could say, I am a lifelong student of success. I sought to understand the difference between those who were able to materialize their ideas, goals, and visions, and those who could only talk or dream about them.

I discovered the difference between them has nothing to do with working harder, although some great achievers do. It has nothing to do with being smarter either, although some are. It has nothing to do with being a better or more "righteous" person, although some are that as well. I discovered principles anyone can learn and actualize through what I now refer to as IMC. And yes, the depth of one's desire, conviction, and even more importantly, their willingness to suspend disbelief plays a large role.

Remember, to have something you have never had before, you have to do something you have never done before! So, if your dreams for tomorrow are greater than where you are today, what are you willing to do to achieve them?

One of the most exciting periods in my career occurred during the mid-'80s to mid-'90s at General Electric (GE), working with Jack Welch at the helm. I felt like I had arrived! My career was off to a great start, and I had a clear path for continued advancement. Creativity and innovation were celebrated, encouraged, and rewarded. Bureaucratic machinations were not tolerated. Jack's motto for General Electric was straightforward: speed, simplicity, self-confidence. I had no problem adopting that motto as my own and promoting it across the business division I led.

Two inflection points impacted my predictable rise-to-the-top career. The first came when Jack announced that every business in the GE portfolio—including the one I worked in—would reach number one or number two in their particular market within three years or they would be removed from the GE portfolio.

Although none of the businesses were told how to achieve that audacious goal, they had some guiding principles. They were given resources, time, and a forum to voice opportunities for improvement. It wasn't good enough to merely generate bottom line results; it was equally important to demonstrate the values behind the mechanisms that achieved those results.

People were important too. Everyone across each business in the GE portfolio was involved. And we were doing great; the business seemed to be growing. That said, unfortunately, the business I worked in only made it to number three in our market.

That marked the second inflection point in my corporate career. Jack announced the business I had so carefully planned my career around was being sold. So much for my predictable future. How could this happen after I had given so much?

As I spent time coming to grips with what came next for me, I recognized the cornerstone of what would become IMC: the courage to claim your vision. Jack Welch had envisioned what kind of company GE was going to become, and he put a stake in the ground. He did not waiver from his decision. He put into play everything that was needed to achieve his vision.

At that time, each of the GE businesses became the obvious choice in their market. In most cases, they defined the market by becoming the "one and only." Other businesses could only do their best to emulate GE's success and carve out a small piece of the market for themselves— sort of like being relegated to the back of the line.

Principles of IMC

Those pivotal moments and my innate curiosity led me to create IMC principles. Through these principles, IMC creates the revolutionary paradigm shift you need to transcend the status quo. It takes you and your business from where you are today to experience the monumental impact you want to make, leading with clarity and certainty, a new ethos, mindset, and process.

The six core, quantum growth-accelerating practices of IMC will propel your leadership to new heights. Through the consistent implementation of the IMC principles, it is possible to move from chaos, indecision, and paralysis by analysis toward definitive decisions and consistent action in the right direction. You'll learn to do it all with speed, simplicity, and self-confidence.

Remember, the best way to predict the future is to CREATE it. So, let's start creating our future together with the six IMC principles!

Principle #1: Courage of Claim

Go beyond the traditional vision-setting, goal-setting process to state and stake your claim for what you are creating in the world. Consistently communicate your goal. By doing so, you're exhibiting your Courage of Claim. Its potency will draw the people and resources you need to bring it to life. Create your own market niche and become the "one and only." Be the icon, the obvious choice.

Having a vision is a must, however, having a vision with a declaration of claim and potency is what will get you through the times when things do not look like they are going in the right direction. Your emotional connection and congruency with your vision is key to connect to the wisdom you need to make that vision a reality.

When this is your starting point, the question becomes, "What must have happened for me [us/our business] to achieve this?" That is a far more powerful question than the typical one of "How do we get there?" It bypasses all the limited thinking, market analysis, studies, competitive assessments, the time-consuming and costly strategic planning so intrinsic to bureaucracy.

There is still a place for some of those methodologies with IMC, however, these days, most businesses have their approach upside down. They try to interpret the marketplace and then determine where to make their play. On the other hand, IMC leaders—mavericks—are too occupied creating the world around their vision! And their vision is infused with their unwavering Courage of Claim and potency for life. They have taken the introspective journey to overcome the fear of change, the fear of looking foolish, and the fear of failure. They have turned fear aside to discover what may be possible.

Infuse your claim with heartfelt commitment, passion, and potency. It will then become, quite literally, a transmission that draws the very people and resources you need to turn your vision into a reality.

Principle #2: Your Moment of Truth

All too often, when we dream about our visions, they are distant. We think "someday" they will materialize. In the world of IMC, "someday" equates to "never"! Action must be taken to turn "someday" into "today." Rather than dream about it, vividly imagine your Moment of Truth.

Your Moment of Truth is the exact moment, with specific evidence, you'll arrive at that place where you know your goal is realized. So rather than envisioning your business being sold so you can sail off into the sunset, identify the event that demonstrates to you—with absolute certainty—that the event occurred. For example, envision yourself doing something specific with the money acquired through the sale of your business.

Leaders trained in the concepts of IMC have learned to live as though their vision, and their Moment of Truth, is already their reality. They hold the emotional state of that reality. You can do the same. Identify your Moment of Truth and locate yourself in that specific event. See, feel, and operate as if your future vision has already happened. Act and lead from that state of awareness as though it is accomplished.

As a student of the sciences and ancient wisdom practices, I'm a provocateur and illuminator. I have studied and tested this principle for myself and with a number of my most skeptical clients only to prove its consistent outcome time and time again. I can explain it by blending the latest proven neuroscience techniques with ancient wisdom and the extreme "possibility thinking" of the most renegade mavericks on the planet. However, until you do it for yourself—remembering to suspend your disbelief—you will never understand the absolute power of this principle.

Principle #3: Dual Awareness

This is a phenomenal and powerful principle of IMC—the very principle that supports the day by day, moment by moment incremental steps and decisions leading you directly toward your goal. Dual Awareness is the leadership and personal mastery skill that simultaneously holds awareness of two realities. The first is your current situation, and the second, the state (the thoughts, feelings, and actions) evident in your Moment of Truth.

Today, you may find yourself struggling to keep your business afloat. You may be experiencing chaos and frustration or the uncertainty of what to do next. There is no denying it or burying it. There is no point in blind optimism. Thinking positive thoughts and hoping it goes away or improves, without considering the reality of the situation, only creates the Pollyanna Syndrome (excessive positivity).

Any leader who has mastered the art of Dual Awareness has created coherence of mind and heart. The leader has a clear mind and an open heart, both in total alignment with their future vision and Moment of Truth.

If you have Dual Awareness, you are not the type of leader who blindly gets caught up in the day or looks for excuses or lays blame on someone else, the market, or anything else. You are the leader who observes the current situation closely. You draw upon wisdom and lead from the belief, feeling, thoughts, and actions of your Moment of Truth, your vision fulfilled.

Such a leader recognizes the simultaneous nature of present, past, and future. They choose to create their future and live from their Moment of Truth. They live in the world of *and* versus *or*. Therefore, acknowledging that all possibilities coexist at the same time, they choose without judgement—simply by preference.

If that sounds like "fake it until you make it," stop right there! The idiom creates an incongruency, a misalignment between heart and mind. The mind wants it to be true and the heart knows you don't believe it. To leaders trained in IMC, their vision, their Moment of Truth, is just as real as the current moment.

Let's say today you are the leader of a $10M business and you have a vision of being a $50M business. And let's say your Moment of Truth is the very moment you announce to your employees that you reached the target, and they will all receive bonuses. Now, how does the leader of a $50M dollar business act? What do they believe to be true? How do they carry themselves? Who do they associate with? How do they think and feel, day to day, moment to moment?

The IMC leader knows that $50M leader starts right now, in this moment. It is the very act that puts the Universe on notice to start conspiring with you to bring the $50M business into physical reality.

As you live your Moment of Truth, take action! You will be astonished by the way people and circumstances align and realign to "right themselves" with your new awareness and leadership.

Be the leader who has already accomplished the goal, and from that state of mind and being, you will find yourself making the wisest choices in the direction of your vision.

Principle #4: Inspiration and Intuition

As you ponder your next phase in life and in business, you don't just want more, you want better. You're feeling nudged toward something bigger; a cause or mission that will unify your current position with your vision for the future. As you hold that vision, you recognize the higher level of intuition that moves and inspires you. It helps you make the wisest choices toward your vision, and you trust it more than any analysis or set of logical equations. You understand it's time to rethink how often we dismiss higher-level intuition in favor of flawed logic.

You cannot have the vision, claim, and passion for your big audacious goal if the wherewithal, the knowledge and wisdom you'll need, doesn't come with it. Whether you choose to explain it through science or ancient wisdom, higher-level Inspiration and Intuition lead you in the right direction, ensuring you are always making the wisest choices along the way—even when, logically, it may not seem so at the time. Although IMC leaders can't always explain their inner wisdom, they recognize it and follow its lead. (We've all had moments where we ignored the nudging of this inner wisdom and regretted it!)

Some call this inner wisdom *intuition*, a *gut feeling*, or a *sixth sense*. I call it your *inner genius*. Your inner genius is not just an inspiration for you, but an inspiration for others to join you on your quest. People want to be a part of something greater than themselves. They'll be compelled to follow the inspired leadership you demonstrate as you lead from your Moment of Truth and a goal already achieved.

What inspires you in the present moment? If you are subject to worry or fear, trying to predict the future or stuck in the past with thoughts like *we have always done it this way,* it will be impossible to connect with your inner genius. Let that all go. Your inner genius lights the path to monumental impact. Remember, you could not have even imagined your audacious goal, your future vision, if the wherewithal to achieve it wasn't already embedded in that vision.

Principle #5: Defying the Gravitational Pull of the Status Quo

Extreme pioneers and mavericks persevere, rising above mediocrity and the status quo. They would not think of going along to get along. They raise the bar for everyone else around them, just like the rising tide raises all boats. They are free to roam, and they draw from the realm of all possibilities, returning with the most innovative, wisest, and simplest solutions imaginable.

They are tuned in to their future vision and believe in their claim, with the heart of receivership, love, and gratitude. Their Moment of Truth awaits.

The only approach to Defying the Gravitational Pull of the Status Quo—the deadly comfort zone—is through the power of congruency, which brings an open heart and clear mind. A leader with a congruent heart and mind, who has been shaped by living the IMC principles, is able to fully lead from their future vision, regardless of any external appearances that might lead others to believe otherwise.

The IMC leader holds fast to the awareness and passion for their vision and their Moment of Truth despite any challenging circumstances in the present moment. The IMC leader will not be deterred.

Principle #6: Humanity at the Center of All

As someone who has already reached the apex of wealth, success, and influence—or someone who is eager to achieve it—you're probably frustrated by watching the top one percent take and hoard when they should have a philanthropic attitude. You believe those with great power and resources should use their knowledge, money, influence, and wisdom in ways that empower others and uplift all of humanity. You believe it's time to rethink what it means to be in the top one percent and to change who we have traditionally looked up to as role models.

In my opinion, doing so truly separates the wheat from the chaff. In the long run, holding humanity at the center of everything we do is the most potent and fulfilling IMC principle of all. It leads to sustaining true, impactful change, supporting the greater good of all.

This is why IMC leaders are sometimes referred to as transcendent leaders. And indeed, they are leaders who have transcended minutia and status quo for clarity of vision, courage of claim, and a specific Moment of Truth. They live from that place while trusting their higher-level intuition and defying the gravitational pull of the status quo.

Those who lead by IMC principles understand that the evolution of themselves and the evolution of humanity are not mutually exclusive. They are, and always have been, intertwined. Whatever their vision, you can be certain it is bigger than self.

While all the IMC principles can be integrated and utilized to achieve monumental impact, the core attribute of a heart-centered perspective creates a unifying connection. It separates ego-driven impact from ego-less impact and serves a significantly higher purpose than self.

The monumental impact of IMC leaders is tied to purpose rather than achievement. I call it *evolution beyond accomplishment.*

Why IMC and Why Now?

We find ourselves in unprecedented times. So many aspects of life seem widely out of control, from the growing pervasiveness of AI and climate change to political polarization, and crisis in healthcare, education, and social services. The world is on the brink, and it is up to us to determine whether it is on the brink of disaster or the emergence of something better.

As IMC leaders, we can influence the shift toward something better. With the concern for humanity at its core, IMC offers an organic way forward. It helps people transcend old leadership styles and methods for a more authentic and personable approach to life. That approach creates inner peace and fulfillment and attracts others to it. It draws them from dreamer (wishing life could be different) to leader (working hard to make life different). With the IMC approach, we become role models with the potential for positive impact on everyone we encounter, ultimately creating a legacy for growth and change.

Through the philosophy and skills imbued through IMC principles, anyone can learn to live with the certainty and confidence that they are consistently moving toward their highest and most worthy goal: a vision for a better life and a better business. Applying the principles of IMC neutralizes uncertainty, indecision, the "Should I, or shouldn't I?" attitude that often holds us back. We begin to live as though our dreams are already realized, especially dreams that are bigger than ourselves.

When your dreams for tomorrow are bigger than where you are today, and you are willing to do something about it, then you just might be an IMC leader at heart.

CHAPTER 4

FIND YOUR
"LO SUFICIENTE"

Dan Grech

Founder and CEO of BizHack Academy

My father's side of the family lives in Mallorca, a Spanish island in the Mediterranean Sea, more than 100 miles south of Barcelona. For millions of visitors, the city where my family lives—Palma de Mallorca—is a place to bask in history, sunshine, and turquoise blue water while wandering ancient tawny-colored stone streets.

For me, it's home. I spent nearly every summer there until circumstances both wonderful (welcoming a new baby to our family) and not-so-wonderful (the COVID-19 pandemic) prevented me from visiting for five years. So, when I went back in 2022, I wanted to spend every minute of my five-week visit reconnecting with my family and myself.

On Thursdays, my cousins Eva, Sandra, and the rest of my family gathered for lunch at a little shop that serves the island's best tortillas. Now, in the United States, when we hear the word *tortilla*, we think of a flat round of flour or corn that serves as the base for tacos, but in Spain, a tortilla is entirely different. With layers of thinly sliced fried potatoes and fluffy eggs, this classic Spanish omelet serves multiple people and is next-level delicious. The owners of this shop in Palma have perfected it. Their tortillas are a revelation; there's a before and after in your life when you eat one. They make the tortillas only on Thursdays, and naturally they sell out. Luckily, because my cousins come weekly, the shop owners hold a tortilla for my family.

While I was savoring my tortilla, the shop's owner explained how he and his wife wake up at 4:00 a.m. every Thursday to make the tortillas using a family recipe that's a closely guarded secret. I could hear how much love went into each tortilla as he painted the picture of his family cooking together so my family could break bread together.

As I chewed on the fruits of that labor and his words, I began to imagine what it would take to spread the flavor of this business to the world by franchising. Of course, one location would have to be near where I lived in Miami so I could eat this tortilla more often!

Soon, I was spouting off ideas to the owner.

"The world needs this tortilla recipe!" I told him between bites. "We must bring this to Miami! This would be the most successful restaurant. We could call it *Solo Tortilla*—Only Tortillas. It would be a franchise. All you would make every day, all day, would be tortillas. People would come for breakfast, lunch, and dinner to eat your tortillas. You would have branches in every major city across Spain, in the United States—the world!"

But instead of looking at me—the scaling up guru—with wide-eyed excitement and grabbing the nearest pen to take notes, the owner looked at me strangely, and he walked away.

I turned to look at my cousins, whose expressions said they thought I was a maniac.

"Solo Tortillas sounds like a nightmare!" Eva said. "Instead of getting up one day a week at 4:00 a.m., are they going to get up every day at 4:00 a.m.? Are they going to have to manage multiple locations? Are they not going to cook the food and deal with a lower-quality product? No, no, no! That's not the way we think here. That's a recipe for unhappiness!"

What she said stood in contrast to everything I had learned about building a business and scaling up in the United States. Why were their perspectives, and mine, on what was feasible for this small tortilla shop so different? Still, I persisted, talking about how to produce a niche product that delighted your customer, then focus on building systems and processes to spread it over the world to create a scalable, reproducible brand.

"How could any business owner not want more?" I asked.

With a hint of frustration, Sandra said, "Danny, it's because we have enough. *Tenemos lo suficiente.*"

Satiated

Like the husband-and-wife owners of the tortilla shop, Sandra and her husband run a small successful family business in Palma. Her parents started a gymnastics studio downtown while working full-time jobs. Later, Sandra and her husband took over the business. As a result of their hard work, the gym has risen to prominence as one of the best in Spain for young women, and they often produce champion gymnasts.

The gym is in the basement of an apartment building, and Sandra and her husband have made use of every square inch of space, knowing that they still won't have enough room to accept every student. Again, I saw an opportunity for growth. They could expand to a second location, hire more trainers, and teach more aspiring gymnasts while making more money.

When I suggested the idea to Sandra, she simply said, "I don't want that."

"I'm happy working in the business with my husband," Sandra continued. "Every afternoon after school, my two daughters join me for the lessons I teach, and I love seeing them succeed. My daughters and their friends are going to compete in the Spanish National Championship. We have enough money and a lovely house in a pleasant village with an abundant garden stocked with citrus and fig trees. I see my parents, my sister, and her family for a meal every Sunday. We spend the month of August every year on vacation. We're happy. We have enough."

Those words again. *Lo suficiente.*

Her words brought me to a complete stop. I'm from the wealthiest country in the history of the world, and I can't think of anyone in my life in the United States who would say, "I have enough." Having enough is even looked down upon in our society that values scaling up and hustling for more above all else.

Over the days and weeks that followed, I thought a lot about what Sandra meant by "lo suficiente." Was that just her? Or was that truer of business owners in Spain and Europe as a whole? What I observed from Sandra and the owner of the tortilla shop was a more authentic example of work-life balance than any I've seen back home. While the burned-out coaches and productivity prophets on TikTok preach the gospel of working within our country's capitalistic system to find transcendence, the state takes care of my family in Spain.

For instance, the government paid Sandra and her husband the same amount they had been making from operating the studio when she had to close the gym due to COVID-19. She already had free healthcare, so that wasn't a concern. She didn't worry about closing her business amid a once-in-a-lifetime global epidemic because she knew she and her family were economically and financially secure. She could quarantine and keep her family safe without worrying if she would be able to provide for them once the worst had passed.

It's okay to feel a bit envious of those sentences—I certainly did. I had lived the exact opposite experience. I was so stressed running my marketing consultancy during the pandemic I gained 30 pounds. I had to pivot my business twice to survive and was $5,000 away from running out of cash. I cut back on my health insurance and stopped seeing my doctor. In the United States, all it takes is one major illness to put a family like mine into a desperate position where we struggle to afford necessities like food and health care. (Of course, I am writing this from the position of privilege into which I was born.)

Sandra is fortunate to live in a country where people can go about their daily lives without worrying about whether they will have access to adequate food and shelter. They can feel safe from crime or violence, live and work in a secure environment, and have a reliable source of income with access to healthcare to maintain their wellbeing and treat serious illnesses.

Because she doesn't have to worry about the basics, Sandra can focus on developing meaningful connections, pursuing work that is meaningful to her, giving back to her community, and caring for her loved ones. Raising her children and witnessing the students' accomplishments in her studio has helped her feel more confident, competent, dignified, and independent.

Sandra didn't gauge the success of her gym by how big it got; instead, she looked at how it touched her and her students. Like the tortilla shop owner, she didn't see the point in prioritizing growth as a success metric or expanding operations to increase profits. They already had enough.

Sandra made me wonder: What would it be like to appreciate satiation rather than strive for security and the accumulation of *more*?

Complacency

My cousin Eva's son, Rodrigo, 16, is the loveliest, sweetest, most polite young man you can imagine. He's kind, intelligent, and good-hearted. Like most kids, he plays too many video games. And he dreams of becoming an engineer and joining Spain's version of NASA. After Rodrigo confided in me about this aspiration, I realized I knew someone at the organization where he dreamed of working. I informed Rodrigo's dad and offered to set up a meeting with my contact.

I anticipated hearing the response I would have gotten from any red-blooded American parent. They'd say, "Can you make the introduction right now? Can you send the email?" Then, they'd turn to their child and say, "Your uncle Dan's going to do that for you! You better be ready to respond right away! Make sure that your resume is up to date! Don't forget to send a thank you note!"

Instead, Rodrigo's father said, "No, thank you."

I gave him the same puzzled look I'd gotten from the tortilla shop owner a few weeks earlier.

"This is a dream that could never possibly come true," the father continued. "He could be number one in his class and attend the top engineering school, but he will never work there in a million years. He needs to be more realistic."

It broke my heart to hear Rodrigo's dreams dismissed. I felt confused and mildly indignant. The admiration I had been building for this European lifestyle began shifting.

I knew my cousin wanted the best for his son, so why wouldn't he encourage him to follow his dream? I came to realize that my cousin wasn't trying to be cruel. Instead, he felt he was being practical. His words reflected the widespread cynicism in many European countries about the next generation's financial future. A 2022 McKinsey study found that pessimism in western Europe is at an all-time high amid economic uncertainty.[1] Even in the U.S., McKinsey found in another 2022 study that Americans increasingly feel opportunity for the next generation is slipping away.[2]

Why would Rodrigo's father encourage Rodrigo to strive for more when it would most likely lead to disappointment in a sclerotic economy? What's the point of wanting more when even enough is becoming endangered?

---

1   "European consumer pessimism intensifies in the face of rising prices," McKinsey & Company, Survey, October 27, 2022, https://www.mckinsey.com/capabilities/growth-marketing-and-sales/our-insights/survey-european-consumer-sentiment-during-the-coronavirus-crisis.

2   "Inflation-weary Americans are increasingly pessimistic about the economy," McKinsey & Company, Survey, December 13, 2022, https://www.mckinsey.com/featured-insights/inflation/inflation-weary-americans-are-increasingly-pessimistic-about-the-economy.

Rodrigo and his father, like Sandra, have access to a social safety net that ensures they can meet their basic needs. They also live in an economy that's far less dynamic than the U.S. Many of Rodrigo's peers aspire to work for the government because it's a stable job. Instead of using their safety net as a springboard to discover what truly lights them up, they are in search of a professional soft landing.

While Sandra showed me the beauty of lo suficiente, this interaction showed me the dark side of the concept: limited ambitions. And it made me wonder: can you have enough while simultaneously reaching for more? Well, it depends on how you define *enough*.

The Happiness Factor

In the middle of the 20th century, an American psychologist named Abraham Maslow sought to understand what makes people happy and how they achieve it. A 1943 article in the journal *Psychological Review*, "A Theory of Human Motivation," introduced Maslow's hierarchy of needs, a five-level pyramid that illustrates what motivates humans.[3]

From the bottom of the hierarchy upward, the needs are:

- Physiological: Nutrition, air, temperature regulation, shelter, and clothing

- Safety: Order, predictability, financial security, protection against injury and illness

- Social: Love, acceptance, and belonging

- Esteem: Appreciation and respect for oneself and others

- Self-actualization: Self-awareness and the pursuit of fulfilling one's full potential

---

3   A. H. Maslow, (1943). "A theory of human motivation," *Psychological Review*, 50, no, 4 (1943): 370–396, https://doi.org/10.1037/h0054346.

Maslow thought everyone had an underlying desire to achieve self-actualization, to reach their greatest potential by mastering all of their talents and capacities. Over the eight decades since its publication, his pyramid has received its fair share of criticism. It doesn't take into account the nature of different cultures and attitudes—such as those of my family in Spain—or how individual personalities or life circumstances might lead to different desires. Yet, I believe it offers a useful framework to analyze what my cousin Sandra meant when she said she had lo suficiente, to help us understand what we mean when we say we have enough.

According to Maslow, people are motivated to meet their basic needs before they have time or energy to focus on personal or financial growth. The longer these basic needs are ignored, the more a person will want to meet them. For instance, a person will get hungrier the longer they go without eating. If your basic needs aren't met, the higher ones matter less.

But a curious thing happens as you ascend Maslow's Hierarchy. Once our needs on the first four levels are satisfied, we feel less driven to accumulate more. We become satiated. This is what Sandra meant by lo suficiente. Her basic needs were met.

But when we begin to achieve self-actualization, the pinnacle of the pyramid, our appetite becomes insatiable. The more we have, the more we want. When it comes to our development as a person—to fulfilling our potential, to finding meaning and significance—there is never lo suficiente. But when you live in a country like Spain where the youth unemployment rate is often triple that of the U.S., and where a stable government job is often the best career available, you don't look for self-actualization in your work. Your higher needs are met through family and community, not your job.

Horizontal versus Vertical Growth

Capitalism, as practiced in the U.S., defines business success as horizontal growth: making more money, hiring more people, opening more locations, and getting external validation and valuation. They want to scale and make *more*.

But to what end?

According to Milton Friedman's 1970 essay in the *New York Times*, which influenced a generation of executives and political leaders with its call to arms for free-market capitalism, a business's social responsibility is to increase profits.[4]

According to a 1.7 million-person global Gallup survey, people can be content earning between $60,000 and $95,000 per year.[5] In fact, in some regions, having more money is associated with worse satisfaction. That's why some entrepreneurs who sell their businesses and achieve financial freedom feel unfulfilled. Limiting our metrics of success to dollar signs or percentage increases—key markers of horizontal growth—can be a roadmap to emptiness.

Scaling a business in the traditional sense is about horizontal growth, it's about *more*. But I believe entrepreneurs seeking meaning in their work should use a vertical metaphor for scaling, namely scaling a mountain—as in climbing Maslow's hierarchy of needs to its summit.

In 1970, Maslow expanded his original hierarchy by adding three more needs at the top of his pyramid, bringing the total to eight.

1. Cognitive: Knowledge, exploration, understanding, learning

2. Aesthetic: Creativity, beauty and form, music, art, literature

3. Transcendence: Finding meaning, helping others, spirituality

---

4   Milton Friedman, "A Friedman doctrine—The Social Responsibility of Business Is to Increase Its Profits," *The New York Times*, September 13, 1970, Section SM, Page 17.

5   Julie Ray, "Being Too Rich Can Hurt Your Chances at Happiness," Gallup Blog, February 27, 2018, https://news.gallup.com/opinion/gallup/228278/rich-hurt-chances-happiness.aspx.

This is the essence of vertical growth. The concept of scaling in business is redefined as using entrepreneurship to achieve self-actualization: knowledge, creativity, and transcendence.

As an entrepreneur seeking purposeful work, scaling a business should mean scaling the hierarchy of needs. After climbing those first four levels and finding security, safety, community, and profitability, it's natural to bask in the sense of accomplishment. Because it *is* an accomplishment. After all, almost two-thirds of businesses fail within the first 10 years.

When a mountaineer begins to ascend, the tree line can obscure the actual peak of the climb. Only after going beyond the edge of the area where trees can grow can the alpinist see the true summit of their trek. Too many entrepreneurs believe they have scaled Mount Everest when all they have done is gotten to base camp. Obstructed vision and self-imposed limitations keep them from achieving their full potential and finding greater fulfilment in their work.

Purpose-Driven Work

What Maslow called self-actualization includes purpose-driven work. When you can integrate your work with who you are and what you believe in—and make the world better—you can transform your business and your life. The more you get of that, the more you want. You go from satiated to insatiable. This is where lo suficiente gives way to something deeper and even more profound.

How do you achieve vertical growth? You identify your core values and learn to distinguish those from limiting beliefs about what you can and can't do.

What are core values?

Whether you're an employer, an employee, or a freelancer, your work is guided by your personal core values. These are the principles that guide your actions and are an essential part of who you are; they were true yesterday and will be true tomorrow. Defining your core values is an essential first step in scaling Maslow's summit.

Some examples of core values include:

- Accountability
- Adventure
- Altruism
- Animal Rights
- Anti-Racism
- Balance
- Change the World
- Chase Your Dreams
- Clear Communication
- Compassion
- Courage
- Creativity
- Dedication to the Excellence
- Deep Connections
- Dependability
- Emotional Intelligence
- Encouragement
- Environmental Protection
- Experimentation
- Extraordinary Experiences
- Fairness
- Family First
- Freedom
- Friendship
- Generosity
- Gratitude
- Growth Mindset
- Happiness
- Harmony
- Honesty
- Honor
- Hope
- Humility
- Humor
- Independence
- Inner Truth
- Inspire Others
- Integrity
- Joy/Fun
- Kindness
- Learning From Mistakes
- Loyalty
- Mentorship
- Open-Mindedness
- Originality
- Patience
- Peace of Mind
- Persistence
- Personal Development
- Personal Expression
- Positive Attitude
- Positive Impact
- Pride in Your Work
- Protecting Others
- Respect
- Responsibility
- Righteousness
- Self-Discipline
- Self-Preservation
- Service to Others
- Sincerity
- Social Justice
- Stewardship
- Sustainability
- Thoughtfulness
- Tolerance
- Transparency
- Trust
- Wellness
- Work Smarter, Not Harder
- Work-Life Balance

What are limiting beliefs?

Self-empowerment guru Tony Robbins defines limiting beliefs as "the stories we tell ourselves about who we are that hold us back from becoming who we are meant to be."[6]

Some examples of common limiting beliefs include:

- I don't have time.

- I need more money.

- I don't have what it takes.

- I'm not strong enough.

- I don't deserve love.

Sometimes, as in Rodrigo's case, limited opportunities can become limiting beliefs.

Limiting beliefs aren't always bad. A limiting belief can be true at a given moment in time, putting useful constraints and guardrails on what we do, but they can quickly outlive their usefulness. Unlike core values, which are true forever, limiting beliefs are true *for now*. These ideas and biases become pernicious when they're so deeply ingrained that they limit our horizons. It often takes someone else to draw our attention to them.

We can learn much about ourselves and our thought processes by examining our limiting beliefs. If we are aware of these constraints without allowing them to pre-determine our decisions, they can serve as valuable guides for our actions and insights. The trick is to recognize self-limiting beliefs for what they are and avoid confusing them up with your values.

Lo suficiente is a useful limiting belief when it comes to meeting your basic needs. When you're on the bottom four levels of Maslow's hierarchy, eating past satiation is gluttony. On the other hand, lo

---

6   Tony Robbins, "The Complete Guide to Limiting Beliefs," Tony Robbins, accessed July 14, 2023, https://www.tonyrobbins.com/limiting-beliefs-guide/.

suficiente may be a pernicious limiting belief when it comes to meeting your full potential. If you settle for merely meeting your minimum needs, you're limiting your potential for development and fulfillment. When you're scaling the mountain of self-actualization, when you're becoming who you're meant to be, then the maxim of Miami architect Morris Lapidus holds: "Too much is never enough."

How do you determine your core values versus your limiting beliefs?

Defining your core values and recognizing your limiting beliefs is hard. Here are two exercises that can help:

- Identify the peak and valley moments in your life. What were core values honored in your peak moments? What were core values violated in your valley moments? Often, it's in the valley moments—the worst moments of your life, when your values are being violated—that what's at your core becomes clearest.

- Take a Clifton StrengthsFinders Assessment.[7] Your five top strengths are a close proxy for your core values. The things you do consistently and better than anyone else are the things you value most. The assessment will not only help you identify your strengths but point you toward your core values.

Limiting Beliefs and Entrepreneurship

In my consultancy, BizHack, I'm passionate about helping build companies driven by purpose that do good in the world. After working with thousands of business owners, some of the most common and pernicious limiting beliefs for an entrepreneur are these:

"I can't self-actualize through my work."

---

7   "Live Your Best Life Using Your Strengths," Gallup Store, Clifton Strengths 34, accessed July 14, 2023, https://store.gallup.com/p/en-ca/10003/cliftonstrengths-34.

"My business can't do well and do good at the same time."

"I have to prioritize my family's wealth over that of my employees."

Those limiting beliefs absolve a business owner from having to do good. They drive businesses to value profits over people. And they lead to unsustainable businesses. Business owners operating at the base of Maslow's hierarchy tend to burn out and their businesses fail, hurting their families, their employees, and their community.

One of the privileges of being an entrepreneur in the United States is that there are fewer barriers to doing well, doing good, and scaling in a way consistent with your personal core values. If you want to build a scalable, sellable company to last, you need to create a company with core values that align with your personal values and a core purpose that reflects your own.

Living our values in our work and finding a healthy work-life integration is incredibly difficult. Entrepreneurs have the power and the responsibility to do good for more people, which is the true reason to scale up the pyramid of needs and take others with us, to look for vertical growth rather than simply horizontal expansion.

The best reason to want vertical growth is to have a more significant impact. Purpose-driven entrepreneurs want to grow to a larger scale because they're hungry to help more people, not to have more. If you can scale humanely, you can be aligned with your values and make a lasting positive change in the world.

Enough, and Beyond

My father was an immigrant to the United States. From him, I learned an appreciation for the innate privileges the U.S. affords those of us born here. Over the decades and my professional tribulations, I've moved up and down Maslow's hierarchy, sometimes precariously slogging through the base levels, and other times, soaring to self-actualization. It's been a constant climb, with peaks and valleys, but my best moments are always when my work aligns with my purpose, and I feel whole.

My cousin Mar is a sophomore at Harvard on a full-ride scholarship. As a Princeton graduate, I feel a kinship to her journey as she navigates the opportunity and challenges that come with an Ivy League education.

When she recently visited me in south Florida for the Thanksgiving holiday, I was finishing writing this chapter. She shared how she strives to balance ambition, vertical growth, and staying true to her core values. Because of her childhood in Spain, she has an innate sense of her version of lo suficiente. I'm in awe of how she's mindfully searching for greater fulfillment, a more profound impact, deeper connections, and a balanced life.

Lo suficiente and purpose-driven work don't have to be in opposition. They work together. When we have "enough" money and status, we can focus on a different kind of climb: scaling the pyramid to self-actualization, pursuit of the greater good, and empowering others to do the same.

CHAPTER 5

GET THE NEXT MEETING

David R. Peters

Financial Advisor, Tax Practitioner, Continuing Professional Education
(CPE) Instructor, and Podcast Host

W**hen I first entered the** business world, I had difficulty distinguishing between my colleagues in sales and those in business development. I was working for a small hedge fund at the time, and to my fresh-out-of-business school eyes, it all looked the same. Both groups met with people who were looking to invest. Both seemed to wear their best suits to meetings. Both seemed to be "schmoozing" with whoever happened to be visiting our office.

After several months of just assuming that the two departments were interchangeable, I finally got up the nerve to ask one of the business development executives I had come to know more about what he actually did.

He summed it up in two sentences: "My goal in a first meeting is to simply get another meeting. That's it."

The simplicity of my friend's words held something deeply profound. While, ultimately, sales are necessary for a company, they are just transactional. Nothing more. They focus on the next transaction only and offer no concrete approach to sustainable growth.

Just because someone buys something from you does not mean they have any loyalty to you or your product. Maybe you simply had the cheapest price, or you were in the right place at the right time. Transaction-based sales relationships are easily broken when the next salesperson comes along with a cheaper deal. Add to that, sales techniques are a dime a dozen. Our inboxes are filled every day with the latest way to influence people or move prospects to a *yes*.

With just the right magical phrase, sales will come pouring in.

All you need is an open mind (and possibly a debit card), *and you will own the sales world.*

The problem with sales techniques is they usually focus too heavily on the first transaction. We want ongoing success, not just one win.

To expand sales, we must look beyond the transaction and cultivate relationships with the client base we already have. We can do that by engaging in true relationship building and planting seeds for future sales. While leading by relationship may be more time consuming than many of the flashy sales techniques filling our inboxes, it is essential and more meaningful than a single transaction. It nurtures business relationships with the best sales leads possible: the people who have already purchased our product or service.

Keep the Encounters Going

To move beyond the transactional nature of a sales relationship, we have to engage in business development, as my friend had indicated to me. This often means looking for ways to deepen client relationships and be truly helpful, and not just sell them more stuff. The goal of business development is simply to get to the next meeting, encounter, or interaction.

Keep the relationship going. That's it.

Many businesses misunderstand the concept. They try to encourage relationships by sending out pens with the company logo, tins of popcorn at holiday time, and birthday cards with illegible signatures. While these gifts may be appreciated, they miss the point. After all, do you really care whether your dentist or insurance agent remembers your birthday?

To build positive encounters, find ways to be helpful. Don't just send clients stuff. Include a thoughtful note about why you're sending a gift. If you're sharing a company newsletter, include a note drawing their attention to content that might be useful to them.

Many tax practitioners send out email blasts or newsletters telling their clients about tax law changes. They toil away trying to get the wording right only to discover most clients are not paying attention anyway. For that reason, I stopped email blasts several years ago. Trying to summarize a large number of new code sections in a concise and easily readable way is a lot of work—wasted time when my clients were not finding it helpful or relevant to their lives.

Now I only reach out to clients about tax law changes when something specific in that change affects them. For example, when the tax law changed a few years ago to allow owners of S-Corporations and partnerships to potentially deduct more state income taxes, I reached out to each partnership and S-Corporation business owner individually to tell them about it. I was specific about how it might save them some money in their situation and how to approach it.

Notice what I said there: I reached out to each of them *individually*, not through an email blast. Admittedly, I copied some text from one email into another, but I made sure that each client knew I was writing directly to and thinking about them personally. This approach took longer than a typical email blast would have, but nearly all of them responded—even if it was just to say thank you.

If you want to keep the positive interactions coming, you have to put thought into it and work at it. There is no way around it.

Any business school graduate will tell you that it is much more expensive to gain a new client than it is to keep the ones you have. Acquisition costs are always cheaper for existing clients. It is easier to get them to renew their subscription, order more of your product, or expand the services they're already purchasing. They already know you and the quality of your work, which means you have begun to establish a relationship. That makes the sales process easier.

Logically, it is a no-brainer. An existing client base represents an opportunity for the highest profit margins and the easiest sales conversions. They represent our largest opportunities for future success, yet it's often difficult getting existing clients to keep buying our products. We have trouble maximizing their potential and expanding the relationship beyond the first sale. They get frustrated and leave, and we are often left wondering what might have been.

Why does this happen? Because we become complacent and settle into a rhythm of simply asking for more sales rather than trying to cultivate true relationships. We become lazy and offer more sales pitches instead of trying to be helpful in areas where the client needs us.

Complacency, Status Quo, and ABC

In behavioral finance, *status quo bias* is the term used to describe an investor's preference for the default option—the option they chose previously. It is the reason most of us make no changes to our investment portfolio from one year to another, nor opt to proactively increase the percentage of our salary that goes into the 401K. In short, we get comfortable with the familiar. Unless we are forced to make a change, we don't. We simply keep going the same way we always have.

This phenomenon can be applied to existing client relationships as well. A preference for the familiar is often the reason our relationships with existing clients become stagnant. As we become too comfortable with the existing relationship, we behave in the perfunctory ways described earlier.

At one point or another, most people have heard the acronym "ABC" or "always be closing" being applied to client relationships. This implies the businessperson should always be hustling to sell his or her product. However, the truth is, an ABC approach grows stale quickly.

This approach does not promote relationship building because it only says, "Look what else you can buy from me." If you hold your client relationships to a transactional level and nothing more, then they will do the same. They will not look at you as a partner. They will look at you as simply another salesperson—someone to be wary of. They will want to ensure they don't get duped, and they will view you as an easily disposable commodity.

It's not easy to build relationships when you provide a product or service where price is the focus. However, it is still possible. For example, tax preparation is no longer a specialized skill. There are many practitioners out there who can prepare a tax return just as well as I can. As much as I hate to admit, tax preparation software seems to get better every year too, making it possible for some clients to prepare their own returns. They know this. I know this.

As a tax practitioner then, I have two choices. One, I can fall into the transactional relationship and compete by price, or two, I can try to offer the client other useful services related to their tax return. The first option does nothing to build the relationship or get to the next interaction. Engaging with a client about price reinforces the idea that my service is no different than any other preparer, and it cuts into my bottom line by shortchanging the value of what I do.

Instead, I chose the second option. After preparing each client's return, I send a personal email telling them what I noticed on their return, and I offer planning suggestions for next year. Those suggestions might include ways to improve their approach to financial recordkeeping or save money, or even a heads up about any anticipated changes that might impact or be of interest to them. Because each email is directed specifically toward an individual client, they know my relationship with them is about more than making a quick buck for preparing a piece of paper for them. I care about helping them achieve their financial goals.

That's moving beyond the transactional. That's creating a meaningful interaction.

Think about what you can do to move away from strictly transactional relationships. Is there related information to the product or service you are selling that the client would find helpful? Are there ways that you can enhance the product or service that they have already purchased?

If we want our relationships with existing clients to grow, we need to move away from complacency and ABC. Instead of the same old thing, we need to start building meaningful interaction on top of meaningful interaction. This requires patience, timing, and refocusing our goals.

Be Willing to Wait

Whether we are talking about job hunting, dating, or sales, desperation is never appealing. When we push too hard for the next sale, our existing clients question our motives. They start to question the quality of our product or service. After all, why do we need to work so hard to sell if our product is so good? They may wonder how many other sales we have made. They may wonder whether our product is a good fit for them. And they may begin to wonder if we will say anything to make a sale.

Any inkling of desperation on our part returns the relationship back to a transactional level. It makes the client feel like a human ATM machine rather than a person who has a need that you are trying to fill.

When I started working as a financial advisor, I spent hours putting together a financial plan for a new client. I reviewed his insurance policies, tax returns, and retirement portfolios, and then spent several hours trying to think of the best recommendations possible. When I presented the plan to him, he was blown away by the thoughtfulness of the suggestions and was happy to pay the fee I charged. In the initial engagement, I had done well. The client was happy, and I felt like I had helped someone.

The follow-up conversations were a different story, though. I wanted the client to know that I could do a good job in other areas, so I kept on reminding him about all the other services we offered.

"You know we could manage your investment portfolio, right?"

"Would you like for me to give you some suggestions for insurance?"

"What about small business consulting?"

I was relentless. It went over poorly, and eventually, my client just stopped talking to me all together. Not only had I failed to win any new business, but I had also lost the existing business.

Expanding existing client relationships takes patience and time. If you focus on asking for the next sale, you may end up losing the client you already had, just as I did. A persistent salesperson can turn into a desperate salesperson very quickly.

Instead, be willing to accept answers like "No," and "Not yet." If the client is not ready to buy another product, accept the decision. Focus on wins that you already have or simply do your best to be helpful. Build on the momentum you already have.

Asking questions about the product or service they have already purchased is a simple way to show that you care about their experience with you and your company. Do they like the product or service? Is it working for them? If they are happy with it, your question reinforces their positive experience with you. If they are struggling with some aspect of the product, you have an opportunity to diagnose the problem and look for a solution. Either way, you build upon previous positive interactions and keep the door open to future business.

Patience in business development can be especially difficult at the beginning of your career when your client base is small. With a new business that is struggling to grow, it is hard to give individual clients time and space. At this stage, the desire to grow means the danger of selling too hard is even greater.

I have learned that if I focus on building positive interaction on top of positive interaction, more sales will eventually come, and the leads grow hotter. When the client is ready to buy, the conversion is easier.

Shut Up and Listen

Academic and business circles have endlessly discussed the importance of listening and its role in communication. While most people seem to agree that listening is important, most of us are pretty bad at it. At one point in my career, before I became a financial advisor, I worked as a hospital chaplain for a large medical facility in western Pennsylvania. I covered three different floors and spent my days talking with patients. We covered anything and everything, including the Steelers' chances of making the playoffs, their families, and the latest thing the medical staff had said to them.

While topics often touched on serious subject matter, it wasn't the conversations about spirituality or life's meaning that I found difficult. It was the listening part. I just found it uncomfortable to sit in silence—even for a few seconds. If a patient would stop to gather his or her thoughts, I would try to finish the thought for them. I thought I was being helpful, crafting words they could not find for themselves. It wasn't until I made rounds with a Rabbi, who had much more experience than me, that I realized how wrong I was.

After seeing my practice of filling in the blanks first-hand, he pulled me aside and gave me five words of advice: "Shut up and just listen. You don't need to fill space. Let them say it. It is more important for them to know that you are hearing them, and you care, than to get the words right."

I was flabbergasted. Before that moment, I had always thought that people relied on me to say something deep and profound and to give a voice to the voiceless. From that point forward, I bit my lip when there was silence and made sure people were finished talking before I chimed in. This seemingly small change was immensely difficult at first, but slowly I started to see results. Patients started telling me more about themselves, their concerns, and their lives. Over time, I began to form real bonds with people. Relationships grew once I allowed people to have their say.

This powerful lesson translates into business relationships too. If you want to form real bonds with clients—the kind that go beyond the transactional—you have to let people talk. Let grandparents tell you about their grandkids. Let your client tell you about how frustrated he is with his condominium association. Let your customer talk about her athletic accomplishments in her younger years. While these things may feel like small talk, you are letting the client feel heard, and that builds relationships. It is a way to keep building on past positive experiences to keep the momentum going.

One of my mentors used to say that if the client talked more than he did in a meeting, it was a successful meeting. The reason for this is simple: people who feel like they are heard want to talk to you more.

Does this mean that you should sit in silence during meetings with existing clients? Of course not. In fact, sharing something about yourself allows clients to view you as more than just a businessperson. It allows them to see you as a human being, which can help them identify with you more easily. However, this should be done sparingly. Dominating the conversation with personal stories may squash the client's opportunities to share with you.

As I can attest from working as both a chaplain and financial advisor, if you listen long enough, people will tell you nearly anything about themselves. You'll hear about their families, hobbies, frustrations, and triumphs. The problem is not usually about getting your existing clients to open up. They already know you and are comfortable with you. It is creating the space that allows them to say what they want to say so the relationship can progress.

Buying Opportunities Versus Hard Sales

If you create the right space for existing clients and care enough to hear what they have to say, opportunities for additional sales begin to appear. You begin to hear how their frustrations, changes in circumstances, and problems may be addressed by something you have to offer. You begin to see ways where you can help.

However, this is dangerous ground for many people. Eagerness to help can emerge in hard sales techniques, and they can undo months of relationship building. Instead of looking to sell, give the client opportunities to buy. The distinction is subtle, but important. Trying to sell forces your agenda onto the client. Giving the client the opportunity to buy presents the decision to the client, but ultimately leaves it in their hands.

So, what is the difference? Let's look at the example of an insurance broker who hears that a client has grown tired of her job and wants to start her own business. That might prompt him to approach her about purchasing insurance for her business.

Saying, "I would be more than happy to help you with insurance for your new business," may go over poorly. It pushes the insurance broker's agenda of trying to sell policies, but it doesn't consider the fact that the client may not be ready to purchase insurance.

Instead, he could say, "Let me know if I can be helpful with insurance on your new business." This second approach doesn't try to rush the client toward a sale. It simply offers to be helpful and places the decision in the hands of the client. If the client was not thinking about purchasing insurance from her existing broker, now she is. The buying opportunity has been created, but within the framework of being helpful, not trying to force a sale.

Whenever I discuss presenting buying opportunities to business development professionals, someone will inevitably say that such an approach is too passive. It never asks for the sale. After all, if you are ever going to expand your business, at some point you have to ask for it. Such a point of view misses the subtlety and strength of a buying opportunity. It does ask for business; it just doesn't do it on the seller's timeline. Presenting a buying opportunity plants a seed. Seeds take time to germinate and grow, but when they do, they bear fruit.

Think about it. Did you ever purchase a product or service before you were ready? If so, you may have felt upset after-the-fact, once you had a chance to digest what happened. You might end up returning it if possible. Or you may waste time trying to justify to yourself or someone else why the purchase was the right move.

Either way, the bottom line is this: pushed sales often leave clients feeling uncomfortable. Presenting buying opportunities doesn't. It leads to higher conversion rates and increased stickiness of customers. If we are going to expand business with our existing clients, we have to do it on their time—not ours.

Plant Seeds but in Due Time and in the Right Order!

In this way then, the secret to expanding business with existing clients is simply a matter of deepening relationships and planting seeds—in that order.

Deepening Relationships

Build positive interactions → Add more positive interactions → Give clients room to say what they want to say

Several years ago, a financial advisor friend learned about proper ordering the hard way. She had recently brought on a new client and had just started managing his investment portfolio. The client mentioned that his father had passed away and he was due to inherit some money. Immediately, my friend went into sales mode. She discussed how the additional funds could be used within his existing portfolio. She mentioned how she could be helpful on the financial side during this difficult time. A few weeks later, my friend discovered that her client had had a very strained relationship with his father and was struggling about whether to accept the inheritance at all. While this was an understandable oversight on my friend's part, it illustrates how important relationship building is.

Misunderstandings and mistakes are more likely to happen when you don't have a relationship in place first. You may not have all the information you need to present appropriate buying opportunities. Conversion to sales becomes easier when you build relationships first because you already know the situation, the people involved, and what the customer's existing needs are.

Recognize the Limits

Up to this point, we have operated on one important assumption: it is possible to expand the existing client relationship. This may not always be the case. Some clients may only want one product from you. They don't want more and never will. If this is the case, you have a choice to make:

- You can be okay with simply maintaining the same relationship with the client that you always have.
- You can hope that they change their mind. (In my experience, this is not likely to happen).
- You can let them go.

While none of these choices are necessarily bad, it is important to realize that the choice is there. The worst thing you can do is have false expectations about a client relationship. This causes nothing but frustration. You keep hoping for something that is never going to happen.

There can be many reasons why a client may never want to expand. In certain industries, expansion may simply be difficult or not tolerated. For example, banking, real estate, and financial advising industries have strict rules around cross-selling and conflicts of interest. More often though, it is simply the case that the client doesn't have the capacity to expand. For example, a client may not want to know more about attorney services if they don't feel like they have any significant legal issues. Or a person's circumstances may limit their expansion opportunities.

Lower the chance of disappointment by exploring expansion potential as part of the client vetting process. Before accepting a new client engagement, think about whether or not a client has the capacity to expand their relationship with you. Will they be interested in other products or services that you offer? Will they need you again for the product they just purchased? Will their needs ever change?

While some of these attributes may not be readily apparent, the more we can think about them upfront, the less likely they will surprise us later on. The more important existing business is to us, the more critical expansion potential is.

~

Your existing client base can be a lucrative source of additional business, but in many ways, the second sale is harder than the first. Developing meaningful relationships takes time and energy. The quick sell is often ineffective and may even cost you the business that you have. However, if we can build relationships before planting seeds, we can come away with happier clients who will stick around for years.

CHAPTER 6

BUILD A THRIVING
WORKPLACE CULTURE

Tom Finn

Co-Founder & CEO of LeggUP®

Fresh out of college, I joined the workforce with a heart full of optimism and ambition, eager to make my mark on the corporate landscape. Despite touting itself as a beacon of success, the organization that hired me pitted employees against each other rather than encouraging collaboration. It promoted those who engaged in backstabbing and leveraged political capital to advance their careers and pet projects. Constructive criticism was nonexistent. Instead, those who dared voice an opinion risked retribution through a variety of means including shadow demotions that might not change titles but impacted their scope of work.

The daily grind chipped away at my spirit until I faded into a mere shadow of the passionate and driven person I had once been. Instead of growth and opportunity, I encountered politics, favoritism, and relentless competition. My creative spark wavered, and I began to question if I was on the right path.

In this organization, workplace culture had gone awry.

During one particularly soul-crushing moment in the midst of a team meeting, I realized I had a choice to make. On that cold and windy Chicago day, the conference room crackled with tension. The chill of the frosty weather seeped into my bones as I witnessed a colleague dare question a leader's decision.

A palpable hush filled the room as the question hung in the air. The person in charge, a formidable national leader with 40 years at the company, fixed a steely gaze on the audacious colleague who had dared to challenge his authority.

"What gives you the right to question this direction?" he barked, shattering the silence.

Undeterred, my colleague stood firm and articulated concerns about the decision, expressing a genuine desire for improvement and inclusivity.

The room became a battleground of opposing voices. Humiliating assaults from those in power clashed with the warmth and determination of those seeking change.

The confrontation kindled a fire within me. Unable to tolerate the verbal assaults on my colleagues any longer, I summoned my courage and spoke. "We can do better. We need a workplace that values everyone's input and promotes compromise. It's not about questioning authority but fostering collaboration and seeing different perspectives."

The person in charge narrowed his eyes, a smirk playing on his lips. "You're treading on dangerous ground, my friend," he retorted coldly. "This really doesn't affect your markets."

His thinly veiled threat hung in the air.

Despite the resistance to developing an inclusive and supportive work environment, breaking the silence was the first step toward change. As I walked out of the conference room, my heart heavy with disappointment, I made a promise to myself: the experience would not define me or my journey. Instead, it would become the catalyst for a greater purpose and growth.

After gleefully resigning from that toxic environment a couple of years later, I embarked on a mission to build a better workplace culture, one that championed collaboration and empathy along with personal and business growth. I yearned to create a space where employees felt valued, heard, and supported, where they could thrive as individuals and team members. That vision fueled my determination and became the foundation of my life's work.

Throughout the highs and lows of the transformative journey that followed, I discovered the incredible opportunity leaders have to influence a workplace culture and empower everyone around them to reach their full potential while helping business grow in a sustainable fashion.

Cultivating an environment that stimulates innovation and progress, while simultaneously avoiding the restrictive policies so common in previous decades, allows people to thrive. This is key for maintaining team spirit, creative output, and growth.

Whatever enterprise you find yourself in, from a grassroots endeavor to a high-level corporation, leaders hold the key to a thriving workplace culture. Every decision made by those in charge, no matter how small, has an impact. It doesn't matter whether you are influencing customers at a local coffee shop or steering a global enterprise's direction and strategy. Good leadership can be felt everywhere; it defines society's progress as much as its people do. By empowering the next generation of workers for long-term success, effective leaders cultivate a healthy and successful organization or community.

Empowerment is more than just a buzzword. It's also more than unlimited paid time off (PTO) and flexible work schedules. It's about providing your team with the necessary tools, resources, and support to develop the competence, confidence, and wellbeing to thrive. Helping your people flourish at work and in life is crucial to retaining them and fostering a happy, healthy, and productive workforce.

It begins with thoughtful, intentional steps. To unlock the full potential of your workplace culture, consider these five practices:

1. Become a role model.

2. Build trust.

3. Encourage risk-taking.

4. Foster a culture of accountability.

5. Encourage creativity and innovation.

1. Become a Role Model

To be an effective leader, the kind who inspires great relationships and growth, you must first ensure your own needs are met. Prioritize yourself by setting aside quality time for rest and relaxation. Delegating tasks or asking for help when needed can also help keep things running smoothly.

Once your needs are met, it's much easier to recognize the distinct needs and diverse backgrounds of your team. Different perspectives spark innovation and create a dynamic environment, so stay alert to the value each individual brings to the table. Whether it's colleagues, managers, suppliers, or customers, respecting and understanding their backgrounds, ethnicities, religions, sexual orientations, and cultures not only establishes successful relationships but adds vitality to your organization. Modeling acceptance and openness to others will lead those whom you work with to do the same.

Leaders become role models by consistently demonstrating and embodying the values and principles they expect from others. To become a role model, you'll need to:

Lead by example. Leaders must show, not just tell, employees what they expect. They should model the behavior they want to see in their employees and walk the talk.

Be ethical. Leaders must be transparent, honest, and fair in their dealings, both internally and externally. This helps build trust and credibility.

Communicate effectively. Leaders must be able to communicate their vision, goals, and expectations clearly, concisely, and consistently. This helps align everyone in the organization toward common objectives.

Encourage growth and development. Leaders should foster a supportive work environment that encourages employees to develop new skills, take risks, and grow both professionally and personally.

Foster collaboration and teamwork. Leaders must create an environment that encourages collaboration and teamwork, promoting cooperation, and a sense of shared responsibility.

Lead with empathy and emotional intelligence. Leaders who are able to understand and respond to the emotional needs of their employees are more likely to be respected and looked up to as role models.

Celebrate successes. Leaders must recognize and celebrate the successes of their employees, both as individuals and as a team. This helps to build morale and motivation.

Being an effective role model is about more than being friendly. It means understanding the unique needs of each individual. To do this, we must take the time to get to know our colleagues on a deeper level. We need to ask questions, listen carefully, and be conscious of language and behavioral choices that can make an impact—positive or negative. By recognizing differences between people and tailoring our interactions based on those variations, we can create a strong and effective team environment that fosters respect, trust, and collaboration. Modeling the right leadership behaviors pays off with improved morale, productivity, and business growth over the long run.

It is the foundational element for creating a thriving workplace culture.

2. Build Trust

Building trust is key to creating an empowered culture in any organization. A culture of trust allows employees to feel safe and secure in their work environment, and it promotes open communication and collaboration among team members. It encourages people to be creative and take risks while allowing them to assume a greater sense of responsibility, ownership, and accountability.

Like everything else about workplace culture, trust between colleagues begins at the top. Leaders are responsible for communicating their commitment to openness, transparency, equity, fairness, and respect through word and action. That includes caring for each employee as an individual, setting clear expectations around performance management, and establishing an equitable process for recognition, promotions, raises, or bonuses based on individual contributions instead of favoritism or seniority.

Employees need to know their feedback matters when it comes to decision-making processes. Leaders should create a safe space where employees feel comfortable asking questions and raising concerns without fear of reprimand or judgement from management. Investing resources in employee training programs can also help build trust by ensuring everyone has the same knowledge base about company policies or process changes.

Creating opportunities for team members to connect with each other outside of work can also help strengthen workplace relationships. Community building further contributes to building a culture of trust.

In the growing city of Austin, Texas I witnessed an incredible transformation take place on a team I had been working with for four years. I encouraged a group of employees to come together and form their own vision of trust to create a culture that embraced inclusivity, collaboration, and of course, trust.

The group began with the simple gesture of greeting each other by name when they arrived at work every morning. "Morning," quickly became, "Good morning, Cameron," or "Good morning, Sarah."

This small act grew into something much bigger as everyone started to recognize how important it was to show respect and kindness toward one another. The changes were evident almost immediately. People stopped gossiping about each other and instead focused on helping one another succeed. Managers provided more feedback so that team members could grow professionally, and most importantly, everyone felt appreciated and valued no matter their background or position within the company.

Before long, this newfound sense of camaraderie spread beyond the walls of their Austin, TX office—customers noticed the difference too! They commented about how pleasant it was to do business with someone who truly cared about them as individuals rather than just being another number on an invoice.

Even better, word got out that this fast-growing start-up had something special going on. People wanted to be part of such a unique environment where everyone worked hard but also took time to enjoy life outside of work hours too.

While remarkably simple, this story is truly inspiring. It's proof positive that even small actions can have huge impacts when we choose care over competition. Building trust is essential to creating an empowered culture in any organization. Trusting that individuals and the collective can meet the objectives of their work, as well as have respect for each other, is key to company well-being and growth.

3. Encourage Risk-Taking

It's essential for teams to understand that risk-taking can be beneficial. It doesn't have to mean recklessness or short-term gain over long-term security. Risk-taking helps teams reach their goals by expanding their capabilities and exploring new opportunities. Because taking risks can mean making mistakes or failing as teams learn how to approach new endeavors, it's imperative to create an environment where failure is accepted as part of learning and growth rather than something negative or shameful. Let your team members know they can take calculated risks without fear of reprisal or criticism when things don't go according to plan.

To get the most out of risk-taking activities, offer your team a structured approach that outlines their intended goals and how they intend to achieve them. Team members need thorough instruction to become aware of any potential hazards and reward along the way. They must also learn about processes for mitigating any associated risks. Additionally, teams should assess their current capabilities and resources before taking on any new risks, so they don't over-stretch or expose themselves to too much uncertainty.

Carefully framed risk-taking encourages team creativity, problem solving, and innovation. Ultimately, if leaders want their teams to take risks they need to lead by example. This means demonstrating how important it is for teams to challenge themselves collectively and recognize when something isn't working out as planned. By doing so, they can create a culture where calculated risk-taking is not only acceptable but actively encouraged as part of an overall strategy for growth and success.

I had been consulting with a group of ambitious professionals in San Diego for only a few months when they decided to further their success by consciously taking more risks. The team had achieved great things already, but felt they needed to embrace risk-taking if they wanted to reach the next level. This science-based startup company was pre-revenue and quickly running out of their investors' money. They had a great product and a fantastic team, but their momentum had slowed.

After some soul-searching and internal debates, they decided that taking risks was essential for them to stay competitive and move forward in their respective product development.

At first, taking more risks wasn't easy; there seemed to be an understanding among the team that risk-taking could lead to reck-lessness or short-term gain over long-term security. However, with some convincing from their younger but talented leader, the team slowly began stepping out of its comfort zone. They embraced riskier opportunities such as hiring highly paid consultants with unconventional backgrounds to bring fresh perspectives into their projects; and pursuing scientific studies in adjacent markets, exploring interdisciplinary collaborations that pushed the boundaries of their expertise.

Additionally, they considered the bold move of going public on the Canadian stock exchange, a decision laden with uncertainties but promising increased visibility and access to capital.

This strategic shift, though uncomfortable initially, ultimately propelled the startup into a trajectory of groundbreaking discoveries and success.

The results were almost immediate. By taking calculated risks rather than playing it safe all the time, the team was able to explore new possibilities and expand their capabilities further than before. Their product was reinvented, and they had plenty of capital from going public to pursue their goals. Messaging quickly aligned with their stakeholder expectations, and the organization went from pre-revenue to revenue in under three months.

Not only did this help them grow professionally, but personally as well. Through these experiences, everyone on the team developed a better understanding of themselves and those around them. That, in turn, further strengthened relationships within the group and growth for the company.

Eventually, after months of hard work and dedication, the members of this talented San Diego-based team managed to not only meet but exceed all expectations, including meeting their milestones and generating funding through the public markets! By effectively balancing risk with reward, they proved that anything is possible when you decide to push yourself outside your boundaries every once in a while—something we can all learn from no matter our profession or industry.

With proper planning and execution, risk-taking has the potential to provide substantial rewards while also helping teams build confidence in their abilities so that they can take on larger challenges moving forward.

4. Foster A Culture of Accountability

For any organization to succeed, it is essential to instill an accountability culture. When accountability is expected, people act responsibly and take ownership of their tasks and projects.

Mastering the art of accountability can be intimidating. Owning up to mistakes and being willing to take criticism takes courage that not everyone possesses—yet it's essential for creating a responsible culture. It demands psychological bravery from those at its helm. Leaders who are willing to hold themselves accountable inspire employees to do the same, lowering the risk of repeated mistakes. No matter the structure of an organization, creating a culture of accountability helps ensure everyone is responsible for their actions.

As Malcolm Gladwell famously said, "Accountability is the mother of all progress."

When I was working with a small marketing business in Madison, Wisconsin, we discovered that the company's 30 employees lacked accountability in their work. Deadlines were frequently missed, projects were poorly executed, and the owner constantly had to clean up the messes. After some meaningful conversations, the owner decided enough was enough and began to implement a culture of accountability in the workplace after losing a few clients to sloppy work.

The owner set clear expectations for each employee and checked on their progress regularly with performance discussions every two weeks. Training opportunities and coaching/mentoring resources were established to support employee growth.

At first, the employees were resistant to change. They were used to working without consequences and unsure of how to take ownership of their work. However, as they saw the positive impact accountability had on their work product and the business, they began to embrace it.

With a culture of accountability in place, this small business in Madison experienced a number of benefits. Deadlines were consistently met, projects were completed to a high standard, and the owner was able to focus on the growth and development of the business, rather than putting out fires with customers.

The employees were also better able to take pride in their work and felt a sense of fulfillment in knowing that they were contributing to the success of the company. They also received recognition for their achievements. With external support from trainers and business coaches, this led to increased motivation and drive.

In the business world, accountability is key. Leaders must be accountable to their employees, their customers, and their shareholders. When things go wrong, leaders need to be willing to take responsibility for their actions and make things right. Although it may be difficult and sometimes daunting, it is essential for building strong and successful teams and companies.

5. Encourage Creativity and Innovation

Championing diversity, sparking curiosity, and challenging norms lies at the heart of true leadership. If we strive to build environments that encourage creative thinking and trailblazing ideas, innovation will follow in their wake. By challenging accepted norms and applauding a diversity of approaches toward problem solving—from out-of-the box ideas to revolutionary solutions—we have the power to push boundaries within our industry. And that inspires growth.

Creativity and innovation have long been seen as the catalysts of productivity in any workplace. From the invention of new technologies to the development of powerful strategies, creativity drives progress and allows us to reach our full potential. As such, it is vital that leaders and managers strive to foster organization cultures encouraging creativity. Doing so makes it possible for employees to tap into their inventive skills.

Years ago, I started working with a San Francisco based healthcare startup. The company was founded by a group of young entrepreneurs who believed that creative and innovative thinking were the lifeblood of any organization. They were determined to build a new type of technology-based healthcare company that not only generated high revenues but also had a unique culture fostering innovation and creativity.

The early days were filled with challenges as the CEO learned the complexities of the healthcare system. The team had to work long hours, hustle to win over customers, and make tough decisions to keep the company afloat. But despite all of this, they never lost sight of their vision. They knew that if they could keep their focus on innovative thinking, they could succeed where others had failed in lowering healthcare costs and providing clinical access to more Americans.

The team consistently pushed the boundaries of what was possible, and their unique approach to problem-solving attracted top talent from around the world. The company's revenues grew year after year, and they quickly became one of the most valuable startups in the tech industry focused on a healthcare revolution.

But the real magic was the culture they had built internally, not necessarily the technology or healthcare delivery system. Employees were encouraged to bring their creativity to work each day, and they were given the freedom to experiment and try new things. This fostered an environment where innovative ideas were born and encouraged, and the company was able to continuously improve and evolve.

By recognizing creative and innovative thinking as the key drivers of their success, they built a company able to continually improve and thrive. And they serve as a shining example to others of what is possible when a company sticks with what works well.

Creative and innovative-thinking power organization revenues as well as foster unique cultures. By investing in new ideas, organizations have the capacity to thrive and progress beyond their original goals.

As leaders, it is our duty to encourage divergent thinking and stir the pot of conventional wisdom. With a commitment to inclusivity and open-mindedness, we can create environments that foster creativity, innovation, and progress.

Lead Your Workplace Culture

Great teams and thriving workplaces don't just happen. They require attention, effort, and commitment. That begins with leaders who are willing to set standards of behavior embodying mutual respect and appreciation. Strive to model these values in your own interactions and set expectations for trust among members of your team. Developing a sense of connection between the members of a team can also be accomplished by dedicating time to social gatherings or team-building activities such as group lunches or game nights. These moments allow employees to get to know one another outside of work dynamics and build relationships based on common interests.

Leaders should ensure that each team member is aware of their role. Regular check-ins and one-on-one meetings support this approach, as does creating an open flow of communication between all team members. Clear expectations ensure everyone is working toward the same goals with shared objectives. It also allows staff to feel confident in their roles while knowing management will be supportive when they need assistance. Setting realistic goals with well-defined timelines and achievable outcomes, ahead of time, builds up mutual respect amongst both parties, which leads to increased trust within the company—essential elements for creating an empowered culture in any organization.

Sustainable growth is essential to the success of any endeavor, big or small. From a local coffee shop to an international corporation, how you implement your talent strategies and communicate with others can make or break the organization. Therefore, it's important for everyone at every level in society—from CEOs to baristas—to support cultural transformation.

CHAPTER 7

THE NEW COMMUNITY-
FIRST MARKETING FUNNEL

Liz Lathan and Nicole Osibodu

Co-Founders of The Community Factory

The connection economy is the economy of prosperity, collaboration, and infinite possibilities. It's the vision of an economic ecosystem, a complex network of interconnected systems built on trust, value alignment, and reciprocity.
– Peace Mitchell, Forbes Business Council

Sorry to destroy your marketing plan, but spending money on pay-per-click banner ads and stock video content no longer serves your company. It doesn't draw people in with the genuine sense of caring that gives them a sense of personal connection to your company.

After suffering through two long pandemic years of isolation, people craved connection. Successful companies—including the world's largest brands—tapped into that craving and discovered that a connected community is the driving force of the new economy. Connection not only builds trust but actually fuels growth—and profits—in a healthy and organic way.

As a result, the marketing funnel is evolving. Proactive companies are evolving their strategies right along with it.

Beginning over a century ago, funnels focused on product first. *Awareness, consideration,* and *purchase* were the key drivers in messaging. In 2010, funnels went *customer-first.* Content marketing efforts focused on the buyer's journey of *discover, learn, try,* and *buy,* leading to *loyalty* and turning fans into *advocates.* If you've evolved from the late-1900s, this is probably the approach you're using now.

Today, about a quarter century later, you should be using or moving toward a *community-first* funnel and reimagining resources to leverage the power of community to drive profits.

If you're unsure of which approach you're currently using, here's a breakdown:

A product-first approach anchors on "push" marketing, which means pushing out content and sales offers to your target customers. A customer-first approach uses a "pull" strategy, inviting your customers to interact with your content and your brand so you can move them further down the funnel. This is probably what you're using right now.

But you'll find the fastest path to growth by taking a community-first approach to the funnel. Activate and arm your employees, prospects, and customers to share the stories they have with your company, and you'll activate a flywheel that keeps team members gainfully employed, prospects coming in the door, and customers sharing their successes.

The **Evolution** of the **Marketing Funnel**

Product-First →	Customer-First →	Community-First [*]
PUSH	PULL	COLLABORATE
Paid Search, Paid Ads, Email List Purchase	Lead magnets, Tradeshows, Advertising	**The Show** (DISCOVERY)
		The Site (LEARN)
Website, Blog, White Pages, Demos	Retargeting, Email Nuture, Events	
		The Series of Gatherings (TRY)
Discounts, Coupons, Promotions	Executive Briefings, Sales Dinners	**The Sounding Board** (BUY)
Loyalty Program, Swag	Customer Sucess, Customer Marketing, Account Based Marketing	**The Shareable Moment** (LOYALTY AND ADVOCACY)

Community First

The community funnel has five parts: *The Show* (Discovery), *The Site* (Learn), *The Series of Gatherings* (Try), *The Sounding Board* (Buy), and *The Shareable Moment* (Loyalty and Advocacy). Design a community funnel for your business by working through a series of five questions:

What is your top-of-funnel mechanism to engage current community members and attract new ones? (The Show.)

The awareness/discovery level sits at the top of the funnel. We call it *The Show*. At this level, your goal is to use your content to leverage fans and create an audience.

The makeup brand Sephora uses YouTube, along with other social media channels, to drive awareness and education. Their YouTube channel has over 1.3M subscribers. Their TikTok channel has over 400K subscribers (with some posts generating up to 4M views), and their Instagram account has more than 21M followers.

The all-time favorite building block brand, LEGO®, has only recently mastered the art of The Show when they went mainstream with the LEGO Masters show on Fox. Season two garnered an average of 3.5M viewers and increased sales by 89% just on eBay alone![1] In 2021, the company revealed that it experienced 27% year-over-year growth.[2] (And none of this even considers the four great LEGO movies released between 2014 and 2019.[3])

But you don't have to be on TV to have a show. Ever heard of MrBeast? This YouTube star has over 100M subscribers. He built an entire fan community around the idea of giving things away in an entertaining way—all by the time he was in his early twenties.

Share customer success stories, best practices, current conversation trends, and other engaging content through a regular podcast or a social media show (like YouTube or TikTok, or even Instagram Reels). Or provide a fantastic regular cadence of written content on Medium or in relevant industry publications.

By drawing your fans in closer, you can nudge them down to the next level of the funnel.

Where will your community members go to find out what's happening? (The Site.)

You could draw community members together through an online platform or just create a web page where your followers can find out what's happening and engage with your community. Either way, *The Site* is an important way for your people to find their people.

In 2017, Sephora launched an online community, which today is one of the world's largest beauty forums with more than 3M members.

---

1   As reported by *Ad News*, https://www.adnews.com.au/news/lego-sales-spike-as-ebay-build-on-nine-s-lego-masters-success.

2   Per the LEGO annual report, https://www.lego.com/en-us/aboutus/news/2022/march/2021-annual-results.

3   The four movies include: *The LEGO Movie*, directed by Phil Lord and Christopher Miller (Warner Animation Group et al., 2014); *The LEGO Batman Movie*, directed by Chris McKay (Warner Animation Group et al., 2017); *The LEGO Ninjago Movie*, directed by Charlie Bean (Warner Animation, 2017); and *The LEGO Movie 2: The Second Part*, directed by Peter Wier (Warner Animation Group et al., 2019).

They use their platform for groups, conversations, photo galleries, and to announce upcoming events.

The LEGO online community has over a million members who want to share their passion and hosts more than 10,000 sellers in over 70 countries. Inside their site, they offer activities, challenges, discussion forums, and parts exchanges. They have a specific area for product ideas, just for their community members to contribute to.

In addition to his YouTube channel (where most of his community resides), MrBeast hosts an active Discord channel with nearly 500K users where he shares announcements. He has 10M followers on his Facebook page, 16M followers on Twitter, and 50M followers on TikTok. However, his most impactful site is called Beast Philanthropy.[4] This is the home of MrBeast. It explains his *why*, his impact, and how companies and followers can get involved to help make the world a better place.

If you're a small business or consulting practice, you might decide that a landing page is the best way to share information. You might choose to launch a Slack channel where customers and prospects can connect with each other after a course you've offered or an event you've hosted.

Important: this is a two-way conversation.

Your website acts as a digital business card or catalog for purchases. It should prioritize information that will educate and convert visitors. But community-enabled sites easily let their community know how they can personally engage with you and others. Where can they watch your show? When can they attend your next gathering? Is there a way to be a part of your inner circle? What resources are available for them to share with others?

All of this information should be readily available on your site. The type of site you need—whether a website, landing page, Slack channel, or an online forum—depends on the objectives of your community. If

---

4   https://www. beastphilanthropy.org

your prospects and customers can't figure out how to engage with you beyond the generic "Contact Us" form on your website, you're doing it wrong.

What kind of gatherings will you provide to bring your community together? (The Series of Gatherings)

The hallmark of any great community is *The Gatherings*. Whether in-person or virtual, your community wants to get together. Consider how often you'll meet and your intended purpose for each event. Don't make the mistake of bringing them together and just turning it into another show, though—don't simply "present" to them for hours. If they just want to consume content, they can do that through your primary show.

Instead, use your gatherings as a time to help community members connect with each other and with you. Ensure you have enough staff present to contribute to the conversation and to build stronger relationships with prospects and clients.

In our opinion, this is the number one most important part of your Community FUNnel. Bringing your community together for energy, camaraderie, and FUN is what this life—and the Hokey Pokey—are all about.

Sephora does so many in-person and virtual events that they have an entire Sephora Events web page.[5] From online influencer launches and collabs, to in-person tutorials at local stores, to celebrity stylists hosting gatherings, Sephora embraces the power of the gathering.

Because LEGO was meant to be played with, it makes perfect sense that, in addition to their in-person amusement parks, LEGOLAND, they would hit the road with community events like the Brick Fest Live roadshow, bringing giant brick pits to the masses. Their community site highlights opportunities for local building groups to gather, and other events that feature their community.

---

5   https://www.sephora-events.com/

MrBeast knows how to bring his crowd together. He opened a burger joint in New Jersey and attracted more than 10K hungry—and excited—customers. His videos are often gatherings in and of themselves, like when he invited 100 subscribers to a private island to compete against each other to WIN the private island!

A small business or consulting practice might host community happy hours and get-togethers, or perhaps develop a series of workshops or other events at industry gatherings. It's even possible to continue to grow the community virtually through online events and video conference collaboration sessions. The key work is *host*. A host does not talk at them the entire time to try and sell anything or manage logistics. A host is there to welcome them in, introduce them to others, and set the tone. Leverage these gatherings to capture content. Onsite video or podcast recording sessions are a great way to amplify conversations to a broader audience through your show.

Remember, the best gatherings don't ask for your customers' time; they give your customers the time of their lives.

What kind of inner circle does your community need? (The Sounding Board)

Your *Sounding Board* could be comprised of a small group of members to have intimate conversations with or to act as a community advisory board. They can help you make sure you always have the pulse of the broader community.

Or you could go for something larger. Sephora is well-known for its Sephora Beauty Insiders program, which gives insiders access to rewards, discounts, gifts, and access to special events and invitations. On occasion, Insiders also get invitations to test drive new products and give feedback on products.

The LEGO VIP program lets members earn points and discounts, get early access to exclusive sets, enjoy members-only gifts, and receive invitations to VIP promotions, programs, and events.

Interestingly, for his sounding board, MrBeast elected to hire his friends to contribute content to his channel rather than a typical inner circle. Many of those friends have since left to pursue other endeavors, but having that initial sounding board of friends was no doubt beneficial to his brand growth.

A small business or consulting practice might develop a sounding board program with 90-minute gatherings where seven to 15 professionals come together virtually to share their current challenges, get feedback on their plights, and give advice. Having an odd number of people is important to avoid any ties on opinions and bringing in more than 15 people make the free flow of conversation less likely and participation more passive.

Rabid fans will want to be a part of your inner circle. You can harness this power through a sounding board program that's either used as your own advisory board or peer group. It need not be more complicated than a monthly gathering of customers with a few key topics of discussion. This inner circle can drive your marketing content through success stories, testimonials, and recommendations. They can even advocate for you by speaking at industry events on your behalf. Of course, you could use an internal facilitator, but we recommend external facilitators to draw out more honest and unbiased conversation.

How will your community share their participation and advocate for you? (The Shareable Moment)

There are a variety of ways to do this. You could choose to use branded merchandise or provide members with content they can share with their own networks. This not only helps you, but it also empowers them.

But really, it's all about word of mouth. Companies like SwagHub have it right when they say that merch is how you can spread the word. It's the easiest, lowest-hanging fruit for your community members to show their pride. But Sephora and LEGO aren't exactly selling branded gear to drive loyalty and advocacy.

Sephora leverages its Beauty Insider program to drive advocacy inside the BeautyTalk forum. They enlist their inner circle to write reviews, share results, and advocate for products inside their community and on their own social channels. They also partner with micro-influencers and ambassadors to share on social media and drive impressions through their networks.

The LEGO team has embraced the adoration their community has for their incredible plastic bricks by giving them the reigns. From Facebook groups to STEM initiatives to robotics coding challenges, their loyalty and advocacy knows no bounds. Do they have swag? A whole site called LEGO Wear, offering everything from t-shirts to snowsuits! It's only available in Europe, but don't worry, you can still get most of it on Amazon or the LEGO store.

A small business or consulting practice might build out a swag store with branded merchandise, or simply create shareable content. Their community inner circle can access and share it to amplify their own eminence among their peers. Bonus points if that content is personalized to them.

Your best community members want to tell the world about you, so arm them with assets they can share. From content captured at every stage of the funnel to actual swag they can wear and share, once your fans truly bond with your message, with your community, and with you, they will want to share that connection with the world.

The shareable moment aligns with the funnel we all know and love but has the added benefit of also being a flywheel. It fuels the entire funnel to continue on infinitely, naturally growing your community, and thereby, growing your customers.

You don't need a marketing plan; you need a community enablement strategy.

Community Enablement Programs

Once you've worked through the five questions and the components of community design, it's time to tackle the community enablement programs. That doesn't mean you need to use each of the five elements to kick off your community if they don't all make sense, or if you only have funding to focus on one or two of them.

However, you can use this framework to craft the exact kind of community you need and determine how you will serve them. You can prioritize what's right for you now and in the future and develop a plan to align your community to your marketing funnel.

Now that you know the parts and pieces, take a look at your community, and determine where you need to invest to hit the right marks. At what phase of the marketing funnel will your community best serve your business?

A startup company looking to launch a new product might start with the sounding board, for example. By bringing together a few potential customers, they can get feedback and buy-in from their ideal customer and build out the content that will be most relevant to a broader audience. From this sounding board, they might find their first six podcast guests, which launches only their "show" with six great podcast episodes, but also sparks 10 or more pieces of short-form content that those guests can share on their own social media channels, thus amplifying the startup's existence to their networks.

It's simple math. Gather 15 people together in a room or virtually and start asking them questions. Show them your roadmap. Talk about your go-to market plans. Get feedback on the pricing model. Give them the timeline you intend to hit to make the changes they recommend. Invite them to help you invite people into the next sounding board. Put them on your email list and share updates with them regularly.

Do it again next week, the week after, and so on, with 15 new people each time. In a month, you'll have 60 people who are invested in watching you succeed. In two months, you'll have 120 people. Now think about this: if 120 people each tell two friends, you could have 360 people on board. And if 360 people each tell two friends, you could have 1,080.

Grow, grow, grow!

Now you have the blueprint. Time to build it out!

A Framework for Connection

In 2021, in the midst of a global pandemic, we wanted to discover the kinds of emotions that drove profitable connections.

What we discovered isn't surprising: the same emotions that connect people in any close relationship are important for great relationships in business too. It boils down to creating an inspiring, caring atmosphere in your community where members are motivated to participate, empowered to embark on new adventures, and above all, they feel welcome.

We know that people do business with people they know, like, and trust, which means that business really is personal. Therefore, the outcome we all want from our events is connection.

Once you create an environment for business readiness by crafting an atmosphere that elicits a sense of community, the final puzzle pieces required to lock in connection are the *Five Cs*. We use them in all the programs we create at The Community Factory.

Care. We believe that everyone has a story to tell, wisdom to share, and problems to solve. Caring about other people and their stories, perspectives, and experiences is at the core of all we do. Our programs create communities that are inclusive, not exclusive. Caring makes people feel like they belong, and it is one of the most powerful motivators in life.

Collaborate. We foster a collaborative mindset where participants are free to bring their challenges and solutions to seek help. During collaboration, we uncover shared goals, leading to the co-creation of new initiatives and bringing in new perspectives and ideas. This is where business relationships begin.

Co-create. If you are familiar with theater improv at all, you'll recognize that co-creation brings a "Yes, and . . ." mentality where each idea builds on the last one. We anchor on the tenets of involvement, engagement, and participation. Through collaboration and shared goals, we co-create projects, business agreements, solutions, and deep, trusting relationships.

Converse. We believe in equality of conversation, which means not letting one person monopolize the time. Conversation must be value-based, not sales-based. Only by listening, thinking, building, and refining our path to an answer do we get solutions that work for the people and businesses we serve.

Connect. This is something that happens naturally and organically, yet it is something that many companies waste billions of dollars trying to force. Connection cannot be forced. Let's repeat that: connection cannot be forced. Highlight that rule, write it down, or tattoo it on your arm, but don't forget it. Connection is the outcome of the previous four elements.

We believe strongly that organic and serendipitous connections abound when, instead of adding more stuff, distractions are taken away. When the distractions are gone and the environment is sparce—outside of a stuffy ballroom, perhaps out in nature—people start to feel comfortable enough to become vulnerable with another person. Only then can connections be made. We create comfortable, walls-down environments full of the right emotions, and now you can, too!

Measuring Success

Community has proven beneficial to corporations. More than a third of consumers surveyed by content agency Dialogue reported that they would be likely to spend more money with a brand if they were a member of a group or a community it had created.[6]

In the 2023 Community Industry Trends Report, 94% of community managers report that their community members are contributing to the business in some way, and 82% report that community is critical to their company's mission.[7]

And yet, 44% still struggle to quantify the value of their community, and 55% say it's difficult to consistently engage their members.[8]

---

6   "How to create a brand community: Set up and success" Nov. 1, 2018, https://www.dialogue.agency/blog/how-to-create-a-brand-community-set-up-and-success.

7   "2023 Community industry Trends Report" 2023, https://go.bevy.com/rs/825-PYC-046/images/cmx-community-industry-report-2023.pdf.

8   Bettermode's roundup of community statistics: https://bettermode.com/blog/online-community-stats.

Monetization

Some community owners monetize through membership fees or private communities. Summit, Chief, and YPO are good examples of communities that charge a substantial five-figure membership fee. Others monetize through product sales, like the Harley Davidson Owner's Group (HOG). Still others are supported by the brand and mined for information. When the time is right, communities are upsold. Businesses like CMO Coffee Talk, run by 6sense, or the VMWare User Group (VMUG) are examples.

From a community member standpoint, no one wants to be sold to, yet everyone is looking for answers, advice, and access from peers, like-minded community members, or those who have had similar experiences. The rubber meets the road when a community is hosted by a company that can solve their problem. For example, 6sense's CMO Coffee Talk community brings together chief marketing officers (CMOs) to talk about insights, advice, and hot topics in marketing. They help community members find authentically helpful 6sense solutions, thus making sales without directly pursuing them.

Measure Your Community's ROI

You can leverage your community's loyalty by running campaigns specifically for and inside your community. The campaigns can then be tied to your customer relationship management (CRM) system to track pipeline and revenue, and truly measure the value of your community.

Here are a few examples that you can employ and track:

Give your community members exclusive or early access to a product or event (and measure the conversions).

Offer them the ability to share access or discounts to their network (and measure the sales).

Create community events where they are clearly and transparently demos or deal acceleration events (and measure the attendance).

Create community education events to help community members understand the next step they can take with your company or your product (and track account expansion).

Run educational webinars to your community (and track the attendance).

Encourage community-generated content that you can use in your marketing and sales materials (and track its usage).

After a few months, you'll have benchmark data that allows you to compare "regular customers" against "community members" and prove that the customers who are part of your community are contributing more to your bottom line than unengaged, transient buyers. You have a big responsibility on your shoulders when you try to design experiences for your community, monetize your community, and keep your community authentically engaged.

It's About the People

Community begins with people. Bringing people together is the only way to launch, grow, and engage your community. Put the people back in your marketing strategy—better yet, rename it a community strategy! And put questions of technology last. Technology may be how your community communicates, but technology itself won't start a community, and it is not the key to helping it thrive.

Building community is not only good for business, but it also feels good, too! Our team at The Community Factory is excited to help you launch, grow, and engage your brand community through community design consultations and support your success with our community as a service offerings.

Business *is* personal. The only way to grow your community is to take it personally.

CHAPTER 8

MASTERING THE PRINCIPLES OF VERTICAL GROWTH

Dan Vega

Entrepreneur, Speaker, Business Coach,
Talk-Show Host, and Investor

Have you unlocked the path to achieving maximum growth from of your business at the quickest rate? All true entrepreneurs and genuine business leaders hope to reach the point where their companies' growth and influence accelerate rapidly. The reason, of course, is to create generational wealth and leave a legacy of enduring impact on the world.

However, you can only sustain this type of growth if your motives are in the right place and your methodology is sound. In my years of coaching and consulting, I've seen organizations large and small collapse because they didn't grasp the foundational principles for sustainable growth acceleration. (I've even witnessed the failure of entire national economic systems for this same reason.)

On the other hand, I've worked with companies and countries that thrived by applying a proven set of financial laws and mathematical principles. The exciting yet rare phenomenon that can optimize your business's development is called *vertical growth*. It is the primary driver of rapid and sustainable expansion.

So, what is vertical growth, and how does it accelerate your company's evolution? Why is it superior to horizontal growth? What obstacles and mindsets must you overcome to achieve it? And how does vertical growth allow you to expand while freeing up your time instead of burdening you with responsibilities?

Let's find out.

Foundational Principles and Examples Behind Vertical Growth

As the name indicates, vertical growth involves extending your company upward instead of outward. What's the difference?

A Modern Definition of Vertical Growth

Let's imagine you want to purchase property and grow a business in an extremely populous city such as Tokyo, New York, or Mumbai where real estate is expensive and hard to come by. To get started, you will probably struggle to secure any appreciable real estate. Even if you manage to acquire it, obtaining land in the surrounding area for physical expansion would surely prove even more difficult.

However, you could grow upward with few restrictions, eventually becoming a skyscraper. From a physical standpoint, such growth is even more impressive and impactful than spreading outward.

Similarly, we achieve vertical growth in business by focusing on impact and influence, allowing revenue to follow. In the early days, without the monetary capital to hire people, we could still achieve this type of growth by exchanging our own transcendent vision for the time and efforts of others. To do so, we stop using inanimate assets as our metrics of success and start measuring the influence we have on human beings.

This occurs when leaders provide personal expertise, an existing network, and business opportunities in exchange for the work of others. This approach—a form of mentoring—benefits everyone involved.

Colleagues gain critical insight and experience while the visionary gains supporters for a greater cause and even evades the uninspiring and mindless work that gets in the way of fulfilling that vision. This process lets you become infinitely impactful.

Promote Ideas Instead of Items

All too easily, entrepreneurs fall in love with a particular product or service and forget the end goal is always satisfying a person's need or desire in exchange for currency. Yet, now more than ever, you have to "sell the sizzle and not the steak."

So, advance beyond selling products and services. Ideas are always the more valuable proposition, holding limitless potential. Concepts have the power to inspire, motivate, and elevate others. Once people fully buy into a potent idea, they become unstoppable. They'll throw their momentum into your vision, making it theirs as well.

Of course, you're in business to make money, and you can do this in one of three ways:

The money you make yourself through your direct efforts.

The money your money makes for you through investment.

The money others make for you through their efforts.

Many people limit themselves to creating income and impact only from the money they make themselves. They hesitate to use their money to generate more through investment, or they lack the confidence required to impress others into making money for them. They assume they'll gain influence *after* making enough money. They don't realize the key to growth is trading in human capital and letting others build wealth for them by engaging with your superlative idea.

The power of engaging others with your ideas is visible through Madam C. J. Walker's endeavors. An African American woman, Walker was born in Louisiana, U.S., to parents who were formerly slaves. She was orphaned as a young child and seemed to have few prospects ahead of her.

But Walker was a visionary. She devised the "Walker System," a set of products and techniques catering to the hair care needs of African-American women at the turn of the twentieth century. She set herself apart by appealing to health concerns related to hair care that had not been addressed for the African-American community. She also promoted her brand with a personal approach. Thus, she sold more than hair care products; she sold a lifestyle.

Beyond gaining customer loyalty, she employed a team of saleswomen whom she termed "Beauty Culturalists." By creating a status system for her followers, she dignified them and built leaders who could grow in the forest of her grand idea. By catering to needs and desires rather than just a product, Walker inspired and enriched countless lives of. She made history as the first female African-American millionaire in the United States, and her business acumen was only surpassed by her philanthropy.

Imitate Walker's approach. Sell underlying ideas that are greater than your product or service. Invest in human capital by building leaders and entrepreneurs. Do this, and you too will reap the benefits of all vertical growth has to offer.

The Trap of Horizontal Growth

Unfortunately, hard work and noble intentions alone aren't the answer to growing vertically. Why do so many companies fail at sustaining growth?

Often, they fall into the trap of run-of-the-mill horizontal growth.

Adherence to the Wrong Metrics

Horizontal growth isn't necessarily easier than vertical growth, but it is the easier way to *measure and demonstrate* expansion. It quickly produces the kind of metrics that investors and shareholders are looking for, often without concern for the bigger picture. Consequently, this type of growth is more expensive in the long run, and it's unsustainable.

A common initial element of this pitfall is busyness. A state of constant activity doesn't always result in good outcomes. The situation is akin to a person who has a strict diet and physical regimen but never seems to get healthy because they're focusing on food and exercise while paying no attention to the mindset that creates an environment for improvement.

In the case of horizontal growth, the leader equates a full calendar with being important or impactful. However, being busy doesn't always correlate to productivity. One's efforts could be Sisyphean in nature—forever exerting oneself and accomplishing nothing.

As the classical Greek philosopher Socrates taught, "Beware of the barrenness of a busy life." Anyone who keeps busy with mundane activities will never create an impact.

Regrettably, busyness has become a badge of honor in our time because it's a simple metric to comprehend. If your schedule is full, surely you must be important! This love of busyness becomes all the more confusing—and perhaps ironic—when you consider we live in an era with more time-saving devices than ever.

At the same time, the digital age has made it easier than ever for us to overwhelm ourselves with unproductive activities that bear markers of progress but not the *substance* of progress. You can envelop yourself in so much busy work that you may be standing still or moving backward.

Effective leaders learn to focus on the metrics that matter. They don't simply claim success over any increase in numbers. Let's demonstrate how this barren busyness happens with a typical scenario, one you've surely encountered.

A small business owner starts a new enterprise and begins to see a level of success. Excited by this initial growth, she examines the numbers and determines she can double her income by simply doubling her efforts. She decides to expand her shop space, hire more employees, and increase inventory. Energized and full of hope, she puts in increasingly longer hours, expecting a corresponding return. Yet, when she reviews her balance sheet at the end of the quarter, she is shocked to realize that her net income has decreased. In fact, her hourly worth is lower than ever. Downhearted and defeated, she struggles to understand where she failed.

What was her problem?

The business owner was treating the human experience that commerce seeks to satisfy as a pure numbers game. If she had spent more time focusing on how to take advantage of human desires, she would have learned to be more productive and sell smarter, gaining time and profitability.

You can probably recall quite a few examples of companies and business leaders who have committed the same error of horizontal expansion. While some can maintain this facade and float along in a sea of mediocrity, others flame out quickly because of overaggressive outward growth.

Others can sustain growth and become trendsetters, but only for a time. They lose sight of—or never really understand—what makes their companies work and collapse by their own undoing.

Blockbuster Video

Here's a familiar case study about rapid horizontal expansion: Blockbuster Video. The company was once an industry leader capitalizing on people's desire for convenient entertainment by renting feature films and video games. However, it failed to transition to the digital era and was bankrupt by 2010.[1]

What's most shocking is that Blockbuster had the chance to purchase a young Netflix in 2000 for a mere $50 million dollars—a pittance

1   Amanda Holpuch, "Blockbuster to close remaining stores as video rental chain calls it quits," *The Guardian*, November 6, 2013, https://www.theguardian.com/business/2013/nov/06/blockbuster-video-closes-remaining-stores.

compared with its current multibillion-dollar valuation![2] Where did Blockbuster miss the mark?

Blockbuster doubled down on expanding to more locations instead of simultaneously taking advantage of the online model that excited people for its convenience and time-saving qualities. By assuming bigger is always better, that less could never be more, and by measuring success in numbers, they missed a golden opportunity.

True, there were bumps in the road for digital media, such as the dot-com bust in 2000.[3] But if Blockbuster had listened to the desires of its customers and dipped its toe in the waters to see what was possible instead of literally laughing Netflix out of its office, they might have survived the approaching market shift.

Mindstrong

Mindstrong, the virtual mental health platform, aimed to fulfill a real need for mobile mental health, and by all accounts, it should have succeeded. Again, leadership didn't appreciate the idea that scale is not the only measure of success. Originally, it intended to build an app that would alert users of impending mental and emotional crises. Now that's an idea worth buying into!

Regrettably, Mindstrong rushed production to get as much funding as possible and found itself kowtowing to investors. The firm had to change gears when they couldn't deliver the product at a cost-effective price—a major faux pas at a time when people wanted mainstream apps to be free.

---

2   Sawdah Bhaimiya, "Netflix's co-founder says Blockbuster execs tried not to laugh when they pitched a $50 million partnership — it's now worth $149 billion," Business Insider, April 19, 2023, https://www.businessinsider.com/netflix-blockbuster-pitch-meeting-rejected-50-million-partnership-deal-2023-4.

3   "The Late 1990s Dot-Com Bubble Implodes in 2000," Goldman Sachs, accessed February 29, 2024, https://www.goldmansachs.com/our-firm/history/moments/2000-dot-com-bubble.html.

After less than a decade in operation, Mindstrong eventually sold off its assets, laid off hundreds of workers, and closed its headquarters for good in early 2023.

A Larger, More Flexible Vision for Growth

These Blockbuster and Mindstrong examples demonstrate that horizontal expansion—whether by generating more of the same product or service or simply growing larger—does not necessarily lead to genuine growth, greater influence, or impactful wealth. An increase in employees, inventory, and space necessitates larger expenditures to maintain and support them. Thus, horizontal expansion is unwieldy, causing its adopters to become bloated and lacking the mobility and flexibility required to get to the top and stay there.

A leader devoted to the strategy of vertical growth has a much larger and flexible vision. Vertical growth is not based on scaling numbers, which are nothing more than impersonal descriptors of facts to aid decision-making. As philosopher Plato declared: "A good decision is based on *knowledge* and not on numbers."

Blockbuster and Mindstrong could have corrected their course by taking a lesson from more prescient competitors.

Blockbuster should have focused on the mission of providing entertainment as conveniently—and profitably—as possible to as many viewers as possible. Instead, the company took the perspective that putting up more outlets was the key to more revenue. They assumed that's what their customers wanted. Instead of committing to a larger ideal, they focused on one way of doing things, and that led to their downfall.

By contrast, Netflix paid attention to *how* people wanted to fill their need for diversion. The company transitioned from mailing DVDs to streaming content. When production studios began creating their own streaming services, the writing was on the wall. Because licensing from those studios would not remain viable long term, Netflix began producing their own programming.

Mindstrong had a great idea but didn't count the costs. As a result, the company abandoned its initial mission of developing wearable technology and AI to help users identify and counteract negative mental health symptoms. Instead, it hastily jumped into the app-based mental health provider market just to stay afloat. However, the new strategy was not profitable and led to Mindstrong's downfall.[4]

Conversely, Teladoc Health has existed for over two decades. During that time, it has grown by adapting to embrace technology, offering an app and video services. It's also worked to meet the needs of different market segments. For example, it acquired BetterHelp, which doesn't accept health insurance, but because the target demographic skews younger and is less likely to have health insurance, it is not an impediment.

Now, look at your business. Are you so committed to a particular way of doing things, or providing a specific service that *you* think is valuable, that you're not really delivering value to your target audience and their aspirations? The outside perspective of a friend or consultant might be eye-opening in this regard.

Don't err as Blockbuster did and stick to a product or model based on conditions of the past. Pivot quickly after determining what ideas and desires sit in the zeitgeist by focusing on the predictability of human behavior.

Take Positive Advantage of Human Behavior

Human behavior is understandable, predictable, and scalable, particularly now, with so much information available about brain science. If your concern for people directs your commercial interests, you'll make fewer mistakes and weather most storms.

Compare this from a purely mathematical approach without regard to the human element. In business, market prediction is a

---

4   Roy Perlis, "Mindstrong's demise and the future of mental health care," *STAT*, February 6, 2023, https://www.statnews.com/2023/02/06/mindstrong-demise-future-mental-health-care/.

fool's errand. Unexpected events cause wide and unpredictable shifts. You must always step back to consider the bigger picture of fulfilling market demands.

Instead of pouring money into product funnels, focus on key market niches to create a passionate and loyal fanbase. Compared to companies that try to go broad, reach everyone, and end up with more one-time buys, a people-focused company tends to generate repeat customers with better potential for growth.

Unfortunately, business leaders too often double down on unsustainable efforts that lead to economic crashes. For instance, no one would argue that homebuilding is a bad idea. In fact, real estate is one of the most reliable investments there are. However, the rush to overbuild and capture as much financial gain as possible through untenable mortgages led to a bubble and economic crisis in 2008 that the world hadn't seen in decades.[5]

Something similar occurred during the recent pandemic lockdowns in 2020. The situation created innumerable opportunities for video conferencing software to explode. While Skype had been the major player and should have retained its crown, Zoom had a customer-first approach that was rich in free features and stable connection quality.

Skype sat comfortably in its position as the market leader, likely presuming lockdowns would assure its peak. Instead, Zoom delivered what people needed and wanted, leading it to overtake the more established brand.

Still, Zoom had to continue to evolve for life after lockdowns. Though its stock prices inevitably came back down to earth, it continued to innovate with AI features to make remote and hybrid work easier than ever. For example, it started its own contact center software for the ever-important customer support field.

---

5   Callum McKelvie, "The 5 worst financial disasters and recessions in history (and what they taught us)," *Live Science*, March 07, 2022, https://www.livescience.com/worst-financial-disasters.

On the other hand, many meal delivery services like Freshly seized an opportunity to expand rapidly without preparing for what the world would be like when in-person activity returned. Though Freshly had been around for nearly a decade, Nestlé acquired it in 2020,[6] and they overshot demand by building a large distribution center that declining customer interest could not sustain. Freshly closed its doors in January 2023.[7]

No matter the market or circumstances, the wise who understand the predictability of human nature swoop in and fortify their vision and their fortunes. (Haven't you heard that more millionaires are made during downturns than at any other time? How else can someone "buy low and sell high"?)

If you focus your efforts on understanding human behavior, you can sell the right ideas and meet the needs of your target audience. That's vertical growth.

Harness the Power of Human Capital

It's imperative that you walk away from this chapter understanding this key principle: human capital—not financial capital—is the key to vertical growth. True influencers center their plans around satiating the human spirit. When you do this, you'll be able to build leaders, promote sustainable growth, and expand your vision as others march confidently behind you.

You can use the predictability of human behavior to become more productive too. For example, consider what good you could do with an extra 10 hours added to your workweek. How could you achieve this without burning yourself out?

6   Nestlé USA acquires Freshly, a pioneer in healthy prepared meals, Nestlé, October 30, 2020, https://www.nestle.com/media/pressreleases/allpressreleases/ nestle-usa-acquires-freshly#:~:text=Nestl%C3%A9%20announced%20today%20 that%20it,successful%20growth%20of%20the%20business.

7   Sam Danley, "Freshly shutting down meal deliveries," Food Business News, January 6, 2023, https://www.foodbusinessnews.net/articles/22958-freshly-shutting-down-meal-deliveries.

Utilize human capital. Every year, many enthusiastic adolescents become adults who are eager to advance their careers. These diamonds in the rough are more than willing to trade their excess time for your abundance of wisdom and experience. So, enlist a brilliant young assistant who can easily spare 10 hours or so a week to come aboard and handle routine matters for you such as notetaking, scheduling, and social media marketing. In exchange, you can offer appropriate access to your network, and they will learn from your expertise. Those 10 hours would be a powerful addition to your human capital.

Now, what if you mobilize five such apprentices to your side? You've literally doubled your work week hours by bartering in human capital! Again, that's the power of vertical growth in action.

As you engage in this form of mentorship, remember to be intentional about providing concrete benefits to those under your wing. Endeavor to cultivate them into leaders and imbue them with a vision that fulfills their potential as well as yours. They will be eternally grateful and reward you indefinitely by spreading your message.

Challenges to Vertical Growth Acceleration

Like any form of growth, vertical growth brings various hurdles. The toughest ones are often those that arise from within. Conquer the following fears for growth acceleration.

The Fear of Losing Your Best Supporters

As you mold your interns, apprentices, assistants, and trainees into leaders, you'll probably fear their growth will motivate them to fly away from your protective nest. By all means, let them! You won't be losing out by letting someone go. In fact, you harm them—and yourself—if you hold them back. You will stunt their progress and end up with an uninspired follower or malcontent who drags your organization down.

Rather, your considerable contributions to their growth and well-being as a mentor will build a close and trusted relationship. Even if they move on to other things, the close connection you have won will continue to enlarge your reach.

The key to retaining your relationship and influence with your apprentices is ensuring that the vision you are providing to them is grand enough to encompass their own visions. Think of your aspirations as a forest where each tree has the capacity to grow, and the mightiest trees can flourish. As trees grow, their root systems become intertwined, fortifying the entire forest ecosystem. Create dreams and ideals that give life to aspiring entrepreneurs and leaders.

Ensure your mentees and assistants can thrive under your direction and allow them to move on at their own discretion.

The Fear of Friction

The second impediment to developing leaders who will spur your growth is the fear they may become rivals either with you or amongst themselves. Banish that fear to fully engage the principle of vertical growth.

Consider a great lesson from the well-regarded leader, Abraham Lincoln, 16th President of the United States. When forming his cabinet at a turbulent time in the history of the young country, he decided against cronyism in awarding posts. Lincoln put into practice what he called "a team of rivals." Instead of surrounding himself with lackeys and *yes-men*, he appointed an amalgam of past political foes and allies.

By promoting members from among the warring factions within his party, he could benefit from the counsel of the strongest men in the country. He gained access to a wide range of viewpoints that sharpened his own thinking. With enormous self-confidence, he skillfully tied together disparate outlooks to craft his policies.

Allowing opposing views to enter your inner circle will invariably create friction. However, friction and irritation create pearls. The most valuable ideas will come from those few employees who are courageous enough to speak out with passion about what they perceive to be the best course of action.

The Fear of Letting Go

As you train and entrust others with responsibility, you will naturally relinquish some level of authority over them. This may feel like a loss since you are no longer interwoven into every aspect of the decision-making process; however, doing so will provide you with much-deserved free time and more mental energy for weightier matters. Bestow implicit trust to your mentees to grow vertically. Only by applying this lesson can your influence excel.

Truly, *there is no greater leader than one who can lead leaders.* Top generals must rely on colonels, lieutenants, and captains to carry their orders down the chain of command. A general who concerns himself with the trivial details of a single unit would divert his own attention from larger threats. You must learn to be the general of your organization, the architect of your vision, and the commander-in-chief who delegates without micromanagement.

Employing the principles of vertical growth is much like erecting a multi-story building. The foundation only has direct contact with the first floor, which sits right above it. A building starts and functions from that base, which is the crux and nexus through which all else operates and flows.

You must be the foundation, the root of all in your organization. Upon you, another solid level can be built, the first floor on which other stories can rest. As the foundation, all essentially comes by and through you, but you do not have constant and direct contact with all the levels you support.

It is crucial to support and trust the leaders you train so they will, in turn, support others. In this manner, you can reach for the upper limits of space.

Accelerate Your Growth Vertically

Expanding horizontally is often a dangerous and dead-end path because it does not account for changing times, unexpected circumstances, and the human element.

Growing vertically, however, involves trading your abundance of wisdom and expertise for the excess time of others. Accomplishing growth in this manner has the potential to stretch your success into the atmosphere, where no boundaries exist.

Vertical growth encourages the kind of visionary ideas that inspire an ardent fanbase to stick to your brand. By building your business through human capital and behavior, you will enjoy vertical growth acceleration as a passport to unimaginable and unrestricted generational wealth and influence.

CHAPTER 9

NONPROFIT GROWTH

Megan McInnis

CEO, The Consultancy, LLC

When I first began nonprofit work, I took the name "nonprofit" literally and believed such an organization aimed for a financial goal of $0 at the end of each year. I thought it was supposed to spend all the money it brought in. Once I began looking into the business side, however, I quickly understood the reality about nonprofit budgets. They need resources. They must have sufficient funds to: a) operate on a daily basis; b) grow into and beyond the following year; and c) build a financial safety net.

Every nonprofit is a business—just a different type of business. There are, in fact, numerous similarities between nonprofits and for-profits. Like all businesses, nonprofits must bring in money, pay staff, buy computers and supplies, pay rent and electricity, and more—as do for-profit businesses. Both also report to a board that oversees the organization's fiscal responsibility and votes on major strategic decisions.

Nonprofit staff can include a CEO, though many are referred to as *Executive Director*. Sizeable nonprofits also employ Vice-Presidents,

CFOs, and people representing the same kind of employee titles and departments seen in small, medium, and large companies. Similarities don't stop there. Both provide products and/or services. Both serve clients of every age. Both experience competition, report to every level of government, and are governed by industry third parties to ensure organizational integrity.

For-profit companies operate with the bottom line of profit or loss. Nonprofits are more complicated. They operate with a triple bottom line: profit, people, and the planet. It's common, though not a best practice, for nonprofits to operate in the red for a couple years at a time. As long as a nonprofit's mission remains its priority, and operations are underway or in transition, it can survive with strong support from its community. After financial recovery, the organization should diligently fund a reserve to prepare for the next unexpected hardship such as a natural disaster, unforeseen attrition, or global pandemic.

The number of ways nonprofits grow and evolve are as varied as their leaders. Some leaders take a methodical approach whereas others leap at opportunities. Some organizations grow slowly, and others grow quickly. Each approach to growth has advantages and disadvantages. A responsible business leader usually chooses a variety of approaches, depending upon the objectives.

Horizontal and Vertical Growth

To better determine and implement the right business method for a nonprofit, start by understanding the differences between horizontal and vertical growth.

Horizontal Growth

Horizontal growth expands products or services into *new markets*. An example is a church, which serves the hungry in its neighborhood each night, deciding to feed the hungry citywide once a week. To expand its existing service beyond the current neighborhood or market, it must acquire additional or culturally appropriate food, additional volunteers to serve more clients, new partners to help provide transportation and insurance, new marketing strategies to find where to reach the new clients, and possibly language translation or other services.

Although it comes with increased costs, horizontal growth brings a particular advantage: an almost unlimited number of clients. A nonprofit feeding the hungry could eventually open its doors to feed every hungry person on the planet. This addresses the *people* prong of the nonprofit bottom line. However, creating new markets comes with challenges.

Vertical Growth

By contrast, vertical growth expands the products or services it currently offers into new products or services for an *existing market*. Take, for example, a food nonprofit that already provides children with afterschool snacks and dinner. Vertical growth could mean giving those same students bags of food to take home each weekend during the school year. Although it may need to expand its call for food supplies, it uses the same staff and resources to serve the existing clientele in a new way. It can be a cost-effective way to expand community services and strengthen the organization—potentially in all three areas of the nonprofit triple bottom line.

The advantage of vertical growth is its potential for a deeper dive with existing clients. Nonprofits typically develop relationships with their clientele and use what they learn about them to provide better services.

~

Unfortunately, whether a nonprofit chooses vertical or horizontal growth, there is no guarantee any new program can achieve the nonprofit triple bottom line of profit, people, and the planet. Yet, either effort may be considered successful as long as it helps the nonprofit achieve its mission—even at an income loss. (A for-profit typically cannot afford this approach.)

No nonprofit can continue in debt on an ongoing basis. At some point, its goals must be met. After all, it is a business.

After applying vertical growth strategies to a start-up company, an established company, a young nonprofit, and an established nonprofit, I've come to believe it is a successful strategy for any business—including nonprofits. Let's look closer at how a nonprofit can establish vertical growth.

It's All in the Programs

Just like a for-profit business, a nonprofit offers products or services or both. Yet, the proper nonprofit terminology is *programs*. Each program is a solution made up of the related products, services, and applicable details to solve a specific problem, helping the nonprofit achieve its mission. All nonprofits offer at least one program. Many offer more. Historically, nonprofits begin when a caring person or group of people *see* a solution to a problem. That solution is the nonprofit's initial program and typically how the nonprofit begins.

Consider a nonprofit that feeds the hungry. The product is the meal. The service or program is the provision of that meal via a food line. Vertical growth could mean the development of another related program for the same clientele, such as free groceries once a week. Still another program might include a shelf of prepared bags, each holding three days of non-perishables for homeless individuals to carry.

By naming programs, the nonprofit has the ability to track its results, analyze budgets, and detail the impact of the program on its profit, people, and the planet. This holistic approach enables the nonprofit to determine where and how to operate more efficiently, fine tune or enhance each program, and determine opportunities for additional funders, partners, or staff.

As with for-profits, nonprofits invest in research, product development, and customer service to understand how they can better serve their clientele. Much of this research is conducted when nonprofit staff or volunteers communicate with clientele. Representatives feeding the hungry may hold in-person conversations with clients on a regular basis for an extended period of time—potentially three times a day. Because of this close attention, nonprofits often develop meaningful relationships with clientele and gain an extraordinary understanding of their needs and wants. (Many for-profit companies only dream about this level of client knowledge and research!)

The more any business understands its clientele, the better it can serve them. If the food nonprofit learns about a group of hungry people who cannot walk nor obtain transportation for food while living under a bridge a few blocks away, the nonprofit might create a new program to bring food to them. This new program may have to operate at a financial loss at first, but it may be worth it if the nonprofit feeds more within its community and can find funding for the additional costs later.

In business speak, nonprofits use formal and informal customer engagement to research client and community needs and opportunities. This results in qualitative and quantitative data used to make strategic decisions. When leadership chooses vertical growth to increase the nonprofit's triple bottom line, it serves the nonprofit's current market in a new way through existing resources.

For the sake of this book and its focus on vertical growth in nonprofits, let's look at how nonprofits grow through a fictional nonprofit organization called Distributing Diapers.

Birth of a Nonprofit

This fictional nonprofit comes into being when its founder, Angel, discovers a need she wants to do something about.

Angel is married, has three young children, she and her partner both work, and the family lives in a townhome. She has a part-time job as an overnight nurse in the local hospital's neonatal intensive care unit (NICU). She loves babies. She can't imagine a better job or career. While her first passion is the medical care of those infants, a very close second is her meaningful conversations with NICU parents in the stillness of the night.

Through these conversations, she is constantly reminded of how much parents love their babies and the joy, celebration, sorrow, and fear they experience in their parenting journey. Over time, she has also observed corporate and community partners of the hospital treating some families differently based upon their financial status, despite the hospital openly serving low-income families. She wonders, *Isn't everyone the same? Shouldn't everyone have the same information or access to supplies?*

When driving home from work one morning, she notices a line extending down the sidewalk of a nearby dental clinic. People are diligently completing forms on clipboards as they wait patiently. This piques her interest.

She looks into it online. She discovers the dentist annually offers one day of free dental service to local residents who earn a living yet are unable to afford basic dental services. She reads on: *The National Association of Dental Plans estimates about 74 million Americans have no dental coverage. That means about 23% of the population, or more than double the percentage of the population that lacks health insurance, could be unable to afford basic dental services like cleanings, fillings, or extractions.*[1]

This free dental service makes sense to her. It serves those in need while solving short-term and potentially long-term health issues. It inspires her to consider potential solutions for the problems facing babies and their families.

---

1   On Oct. 29, 2022. *Don't have dental insurance? Here are places to get free or low-cost care in Nashville.* Mary Hance. Published 5 a.m. CST Sept. 5, 2019. https://www.tennessean.com/story/life/2019/09/05/dental-insurance-nashville-clinics-offer-free-care/2155079001/

Angel has an *aha* moment: *Why don't I provide diapers for the working poor in my community?* After all, she has already met several of these families through the hospital and knows of more who do not have the resources to give birth at a hospital. Plus, she considers the cost of diapers. The Institute for Research on Poverty explains diapers cost an average of $100 per month per child.[2] And, unfortunately, "One in two U.S. families cannot afford enough diapers to keep their infant or child clean, dry, and healthy," according to the National Diaper Bank Network.[3]

Angel is excited!

After a few months of conversation with co-workers, friends, and anyone else who would listen, Angel becomes the founder of Distributing Diapers, completes its initial paperwork, and recruits its board of directors. Together, they develop a mission statement, a business plan, and start recruiting friends and family interested in helping as volunteers.

The Ideal Client

To understand its clientele, a nonprofit takes the same approach as any other business. It begins by creating an avatar to represent its ideal client—aka target audience or target market. Once determined, brainstorm the details about this avatar. There is no limit to the number or type of details. In fact, the more details there are, the more useful the avatar becomes. By determining the avatar's needs and wants, information is revealed which helps guide decisions for the best products and services for this ideal client.

Up to three customer avatars are often created for startups, but this fledgling nonprofit focuses on one avatar to be most effective and efficient with its limited resources.

---

2   On August 5, 2023. Institute for Research on Poverty. Diaper Dilemma: Low-Income Families Face High Costs and Limited Supplies of An Essential Good. Published October 2022. https://www.irp.wisc.edu/resource/diaper-dilemma-low-income-families-face-high-costs-and-limited-supplies-of-an-essential-good/.

3   "This is What Diaper Need Feels Like. Help Us Change It," National Diaper Network, accessed February 29, 2023, https://nationaldiaperbanknetwork.org/.

In this startup phase, Distributing Diapers defines its ideal client as a mom, since moms are often the primary caregivers. Basic information for the Distributing Diapers' avatar includes where the mom lives, her economic status, age, native language, and level of education. As a hyperlocal nonprofit, Distributing Diapers also lists the grocery stores and food banks she might use, as well as the public transportation she takes (and at what times), her hair salon, place of worship, and medical or other supports—if she has any.

Also considered are activities occurring in the neighborhood (or the world) which could affect the client's use of the product, service, or program. For example, how are the global and local economies changing area employment? How is technology impacting how people communicate? Are there national, local, or hyperlocal trends to consider? These factors and more impact the ideal client and should be included in the avatar's description.

The nonprofit board proactively provides this and other general organizational information to its representatives so everyone can "be on the same page" as they engage with the community on its behalf. For example, guidance is provided about where the organization stands on sensitive or cultural issues such as whether they define "moms" by biological gender (or not). This information should be clearly outlined to be easily understood by each volunteer. The support provided, such as a phone number (if the client has additional concerns), and the topic itself consistently be fine-tuned and communicated by for-profit and nonprofit businesses alike.

Inventory

Aligning the organizational mission with the avatar, or ideal client model, allows the nonprofit to determine the best type of product for their clientele. Distributing Diapers' mission is "to provide diapers to local working families unable to afford them." The mission statement and avatar description lead decision-makers to provide any and all types of diapers—cloth, plastic, any size, color, brand, and so on.

The young nonprofit does not have the funds to purchase diapers, so its leadership agrees to hold Diaper Drives—a smart way to collect inventory. However, Angel does not have time to research exactly who to talk to, chase the people down, nor try to persuade them to facilitate the necessary donations. Searching her own life's typical activities for inspiration, she realizes that she talks with the staff of her church on a regular basis. She easily brings up the idea of a diaper drive in conversation with them. After only a couple of exchanges with Angel and amongst themselves, they approve a church-wide diaper drive and agree to hold it in their facility.

For the next step in planning out their first Diaper Drive, Angel brings together the Diaper Divas—a group of volunteers with the skills needed for the event. One person is extremely resourceful and agrees to find storage bins for the drive. Another is computer-savvy and agrees to create flyers for the volunteers to post throughout the church and community.

The flyers are a hit! They create awareness about the drive, as well as the new nonprofit.

The first Diaper Drive is a success! The bins are filled with a variety of diapers. Plus, three church members offer to hold Diaper Drives at their workplaces within the nonprofit's first year. This single effort provides this young nonprofit a solid source of inventory and hope.

Distribution

Distributing Diapers now has its vision, people, and inventory. The volunteers only need to look at the business plan for guidance—to partner with others who already serve local working families.

Angel soon remembers the nearby dental clinic with its annual event. She visits its office, talks with its like-minded office manager and dentist, and learns the annual event is scheduled to be held again in a couple of months. They agree to partner during the event.

The Distributing Diaper volunteers get to work. They sort and label diapers. The computer-savvy volunteer creates two items—a flyer highlighting both the dental and diaper services provided and registration forms on a clipboard to streamline distribution during the event. A few logistics people think through and then write down the flow of the event, when and where to pick up the completed form, and how the diaper volunteer finds the right diapers, hands them to the client, and tracks the new client's name and contact information.

People are excited, and tasks are under way. Word spreads about the event. Soon, the day arrives. Patients line up for dental care and complete the forms for diapers. Some attendees who hadn't heard about the diapers yet are thrilled! The people in line unexpectedly name other working families who could use the diapers as well as places to distribute them. By the end of the event, most of the diapers are distributed and the self-proclaimed Diaper Divas are excited about their success and potential.

Infrastructure

Thanks to the new and potential clients at the dental event, Distributing Diapers has suggestions for partnerships. In fact, more are listed than can be realistically carried out by its passionate, though small, volunteer team. The endless potential of Distributing Diapers may look and feel fantastic, yet it is typically more successful in the long run to lay a solid foundation and build relationships with people it will serve, potential partners, and its own volunteers.

Too many founders (including myself) become excited by an idea but are unable to follow through because infrastructure is not already in place. Learn from my mistakes. Make time to develop a solid foundation and build internal and external relationships (throughout the community and with volunteers). As they say, it is tough to "build a plane while flying." Similarly, it's challenging for an enthusiastic person with a clear vision, who is progressing toward the goal, to be stopped to work on infrastructure. This balancing act is a tightrope only skilled leaders know how to walk.

To keep from stressing about making the "right" next decision, Angel remembers the nonprofit board of Distributing Diapers is responsible for determining strategy. She confers with them. They review the nonprofit's mission and underscore its recent success. They discuss and then vote to prioritize inventory, organizational capacity, and distribution while recommending keeping a narrow geographic focus on this county. Leadership recognizes the original timeline and business plan are already off schedule (in a good way!). They are not slowing down. They approve of progress that aligns with the business strategy and encourage Angel to continue her proven leadership.

Priorities One, Two, and Three

With board support and clear direction, Angel understands that one priority is to increase diaper inventory. She convenes the Diaper Divas, who previously worked on inventory, and invites new volunteers. Those interested in staying with inventory agree to follow up with the three offers from church members. They schedule and prepare three drives. Each volunteer will collect as many diapers as they had for the first drive—or more. Plus, with the new volunteer skills and interests in place, the number of drives can increase and/or the depth of detail within the process of collecting, tracking, and organizing the inventory can be further developed. Related activities can also be added. For example, while some Diaper Divas manage Diaper Drives as they are underway, others can plan and publicize additional drives so the nonprofit can reach and serve even more people in need.

Organizational capacity is wisely prioritized. After all, if nonprofit personnel are unable to follow through, the organization is at risk. Therefore, time is given to allow the Diaper Diva volunteers to plan and follow through on the activities. This may not seem like much, but remember, a volunteer activity must be balanced with the volunteer's family, work, own activities, and the inevitable surprises of life. Providing clear direction, specificity, and time allows volunteers to take care of themselves while enjoying the volunteer experience. This increases the quality of the Distributing Diapers volunteer experience, its volunteer retention and recruitment, and results in better programs moving forward.

Angel's personal priority is for volunteers to engage with clients. She considers it imperative for all volunteers to experience the feel-good emotion as they hand clients the diapers. Volunteers are encouraged to interact with the clients, ask them about their new and older babies, answer questions, and recommend other nonprofit and government resources to ensure the family's basic needs are met.

Distribution is the other priority. The Diaper Divas already have the business plan and client suggestions. Yet, the board recently empowered the volunteers by giving them the authority and ability to customize each partnership opportunity as it arises. (This allows the volunteers to move forward with each potential partnership without needing to obtain board approval.) This strengthens the organization, its business plan, and its volunteers. Therefore, the Diaper Divas seek out and then partner with agencies that already serve the ideal Distributing Diapers client: the local community center, the government, and other nonprofits. After allowing for the necessary time and discussion, the initial, uniquely customized partnerships are:

1. **The one-night-only Christmas Gift Shoppe for the local financially disadvantaged, held at the local community center.** At this annual event, the Christmas Gift Shoppe representatives invite Diaper Divas to talk with anyone walking into the shoppe's infant department. If interested, the client completes the same versatile form originally created for the dental event, and the Diaper Divas hand them their diapers.

2. **A children's daycare for working parents located in public housing.** A local daycare agrees for two Diaper Divas volunteers to show up every Friday evening to give enough diapers to interested families to last a full week. In exchange for the diapers, parents give preapproval for the daycare staff to share

their personal contact information and their baby's personal information with Distributing Diapers, thus building the nonprofit's database.

3. **An annual children's clothing give-away at a church-based consignment shop, a local nonprofit.** The event registration table allows interested attendees to complete the Distributing Diapers form before walking through the doors into the event, held in a multi-purpose room. As each form is completed, a registration table volunteer takes it to the Distributing Diapers table in the event room where a Diaper Diva begins preparing a custom-packed bag for the attendee. The bag is then ready for pick up as he or she walks by the Distributing Diapers table to exit the event.

Their "formula" is working! The Diaper Divas interact with the clients, who appreciate the personal attention, at each event. Each partnership proves successful. Word spreads. More Diaper Drives are held. Similar distribution partnerships are added. And the number of Diaper Divas continues to increase. In business speak, the strategic goals of prioritizing inventory, organizational capacity, and distribution are achieved.

Vertical Growth

After a couple years of steadily building upon its solid foundation, the board now realizes it is time to expand. It decides to continue the established and successful activities while adding a new program. After in-depth research and conversation, the board decides vertical growth is the smartest strategy to design the new program. After all, it provides them with the opportunity to serve existing clientele with existing resources. As a result, they keep the initial program, Diaper Drives, and add Diaper Education. This program provides two options: a one-time class addressing diaper basics for new parents and a more comprehensive four-week class about baby care offered through nonprofit partner venues\.

These vertical growth tactics allow Distributing Diapers to build an additional program using current resources with existing clients. Continuing with vertical growth strategy, this young nonprofit serves its clients more thoroughly, develops deeper relationships with them, and more profoundly impacts families.

There are opportunities for further growth such as offering these new classes to the partners' clientele, placing diapers in thrift stores, supplying diapers for other agencies to distribute, or selling a new class to for-profit companies to offer various training programs to their employees. Or the nonprofit may choose to "grow with the baby" by developing programs for older babies as they become toddlers and preschoolers. None are bad ideas. Some may be good. Others may be terrific.

$\sim$

Like any other business, nonprofits can utilize strategies for vertical or horizontal growth, or a combination of the two. However, vertical growth is clearly a cost-effective and strategic choice to strengthen nonprofit programs, deepen the organizational impact on clientele, and continue to fulfill the nonprofit's mission.

Isn't that what growth for any business is all about?

CHAPTER 10

DRIVE YOUR ONLINE PRESENCE BY CHOOSING THE BEST LANES

Ira Bowman

SEO Specialist, Social Media Strategist, Web Development,

2x TEDx Speaker, Best-Selling Author, Philanthropist

Almost everyone with a website will tell you they would like to increase their website traffic. Unfortunately, most of them have no idea *how* to get that increased traffic. So, what should they do to make their dream come true?

Drive in the best lanes.

Let's get started by taking a 30,000-foot view of the six main sources of website traffic and define some terms that will come in handy for the rest of the chapter. Please note, individual results may vary based on specific marketing efforts.

Six Main Sources of Website Traffic

Organic Traffic

Organic traffic occurs when someone opens a browser and simply types in a website address or clicks on a bookmark they previously saved. Organic traffic is great because visitors who take this lane are normally there for a good reason. The problem is, of course, that this is the least common type of website traffic, so it's like a road less traveled. Don't count on it for any major volume. It's hard to survive on organic traffic alone, especially with medium and larger sized companies.

Referrals

Referrals are wonderful and direct visitors to your website in a variety of ways. Referred visitors may click an email link, type in the address someone gave them, or perhaps click on an address from a social media or search engine result. However, the important distinction between this lane and the others is that these visitors were referred to a website by someone they know and most likely trust. That trust makes referral traffic extremely beneficial, but like organic traffic, there usually aren't enough referred visitors to sustain a large website traffic volume.

Paid Ads

Also known as PPC—which stands for *pay per click*—paid ads generate visitors fast. However, this approach comes at a high cost with average bounce rates of over 80%. Visitors "bounce" when they come to your website without clicking on any of its website buttons, visiting any additional pages, or engaging in any way before they leave. Bounce is measured by Google, and high bounce rates negatively affect your website's ranking. Unfortunately, too many people lean heavily on this method of drawing traffic without realizing the negative opportunity cost.

Email

Business email can generate a lot of website traffic, so many professionals include links to their website in their email signature lines. While this traffic normally has a low bounce rate, it simply doesn't generate enough traffic to make a huge impact. Automated email campaigns can increase traffic by targeting potential visitors with the aid of contact record management software (CRM) and through the use of landing pages. In my experience, email is more effective for generating quality website traffic than a PPC campaign.

Social Media

One of the best sources of traffic generation is social media. Businesses can build a rapport with their audience on social media before the audience ever visits the company website. That relationship means they are far less likely to bounce when they arrive. I've found bounce rates are typically around 20% when the traffic originates from social media channels. Social media is second only to search engines in generating website traffic. (We'll dig deeper into this soon.)

Search Engines

The king of the hill, when it comes to website traffic, is found in the form of search engines, namely Google. Search engine traffic can be hard to earn, so just like with social media, the website owner will need to put in some work, or have someone put in some work, on their behalf to capture droves of website traffic from search engines. That work is known as SEO, which stands for search engine optimization.

The Two Best Lanes

As you can see, social media and search engines are the two best lanes for driving traffic to websites without breaking the proverbial bank.

Are you wondering why they rank so much higher than the other options?

A clue to the answer is volume. These are the only two places you can find people hanging out globally by the billions. Simply put, billions of people use social media and utilize search engines every single day. Leveraging these two streams of existing traffic and diverting some of it to a website is a great way to build game-changing website traffic.

Social Media: An Often-Overlooked Gold Mine

Relationships are the ultimate name of the game for valuable website traffic. Why? Simply put—and not to be understated—website visitors who already know, like, and trust a brand before they visit the website are far more likely to become clients. A person with prebuilt brand loyalty is far more patient with any website issues. They will invariably put up with slower load speeds, be patient with an unclear call to action, and try harder to find less obvious information—they are far less likely to bounce.

Bounce rates are important to a website ranking commonly expressed as *DA* (domain authority), so the longer a person stays on the website, and the more they engage with the website, the more they help the website increase its own DA.

Social media helps to build these critical relationships by creating conversations, sharing case studies, enticing the audience with infographics, building loyalty with two-way conversations in the comment sections, and gaining participation in company polls. This lets the audience know about promotions, the use of influencers, hashtag use, videos, graphics, and utilizing other social media marketing strategies.

The relationship between prospective consumers and the brand can start with the business owner(s), managers, or employees. The conversation can begin on the company's website or social media profiles or on the individual pages of anyone who mentions the business in a post by simply responding to a question, celebrating a review, or offering more information about a topic or product mentioned.

One tip to increasing a business's social media following is to encourage the employees of that business to make posts about positive things that happen on the job. I also recommend that employees engage with posts made by the company's business profile by leaving a comment or sharing the post on their personal accounts.

Why?

The engagement helps to increase overall visibility by activating the platform algorithm, and it helps generate a more engaging environment for fans of the brand to hang out. It is hard to be social if you find yourself somewhere alone. Business pages with more activity will likely generate more website traffic. So, I advise business management to incentivize their staff to participate—if they are not already doing so of their own accord.

Did you know there are billions of users on social media every single day? Imagine what would happen if you could siphon off just a small fraction of that community away from Facebook, Instagram, LinkedIn, YouTube, TikTok, Twitter, Pinterest, and more, each day, to visit your website. The fact is, successful businesses are doing just that.

One way businesses siphon traffic from social media to their websites is by being *social* on social media. In the past, many marketing departments would come across as more clinical or sterile. Matter-of-fact posts and announcements were commonplace. Social media channels were used as an extension of a business's public relations department and simply shared cold facts and press releases.

A better strategy has emerged. Now successful social media marketing campaigns include sharing case studies, highlighting vendors, talking about things employees discuss at the water cooler, and sharing interesting things happening in the world. Many of the most successful business social media campaigns are not about the product or the company but include charity work, social causes, and human-interest stories. These and other nonlinear business elements attract people who might not be interested in facts and figures about the business.

The goal here is to enter their field of vision by discussing things they *are* interested in. When someone catches a glimpse of your social media page and finds it has interesting content, they are far more likely to follow or subscribe. After they visit a few times without being spammed by boring messages that just try to sell them something, you'll find most of them start to like your posts and engage in the comments. From there, it doesn't take long to build trust that eventually turns into brand interest-enthusiasm-trust.

Even with all of those good feelings, newly converted social media fans might not visit the website—and that is okay!

How can that be okay? you may wonder.

Many people loyal to a social media page don't bother visiting the website because they already feel connected to the company, right there in the social media space, where the company has built engagement and rapport. A person like that is a new brand ambassador. They will engage with posts and refer others to the business when they see a match.

This happens online and off, because the business is top of mind, and it is one they now trust. The power of affiliate marketing happens here—without the cost. This is free help and can become a huge new goldmine for your business. The goal for all businesses should be to repeat this kind of engagement many times over.

How do you decide which social media channel to focus on?

Okay, so you want to build a goldmine of your own on social media to generate more website traffic. With so many social channels out there, where should you focus your attention?

The first step is to recognize the demographic categories that make up your primary prospects. In the digital marketing world, they are referred to as an avatar or buyer persona. Generally, companies will target prospects based on demographics that can include gender, age, education, race, income, and possibly whether they live in an urban, suburban, or rural area.

Not all criterium have to be used in each case. Some companies don't look at these demographics at all; they simply use a wide net and hope to catch as prospects as they can. However, discovering the buyer persona for your business can truly help create a more efficient strategy, especially if you are looking to strike fast or hit paydirt with a smaller marketing budget.

So where will you find the most people to fit your avatar? The more information you have, the more accurately you can assess where to invest your time and efforts. As of June 2023, TikTok is the number one social media platform to catch the attention of people from ages 10 to 19.[1] It has the largest daily website traffic of any website on the planet—even more than the previous king of the hill, YouTube. TikTok was the number one downloaded app on the planet in 2020 and 2021 as well, so it shouldn't be dismissed as a place only for children.[2] People in all demographics are on TikTok to varying degrees.

Note: these ratings are based on the length of time visitors stay, not simply the overall volume of visitors. Users typically stop to watch a few videos and end up staying for hours. In 2023, the average length of use for TikTok was a whopping 13 hours per month![3]

The number one platform for adults in the USA, with over 80% of adults having an account, is YouTube. YouTube has 2.5 billion monthly users on average as of June 2023, and I expect it to continue to rise because there are over 1 billion people expected to gain access to the internet, from developing countries around the world in the coming months.[4] Many people use it for looking up how-to videos, but with the surge in popularity of other video platforms, YouTube is doing a good job of competing for both entertainment and educational social media visitors as well.

With over 2.9 billion users, Facebook still has the largest single audience, however, they have been losing their share lately.[5] If the trend continues, other platforms like YouTube will likely steal that crown in the not-so-distant future.

Looking for a more mature female audience? Want to find younger

---

1   Adam Connell, "32 Latest TikTok Statistics For 2023: The Definitive List," Blogging Wizard, February 10, 2023, https://bloggingwizard.com/tiktok-statistics/.

2   Ibid.

3   Ibid.

4   Jack Flynn, "How Many People Use the Internet? [2023]: 35 Facts About Internet Usage in America and the World," Zippia, January 12, 2023, https://www.zippia.com/advice/how-many-people-use-the-internet/.

5   "Number of monthly active Facebook users worldwide as of 1st quarter 2023," Statista, April 2023, https://www.statista.com/statistics/264810/number-of-monthly-active-facebook-users-worldwide/.

males who mostly live in an urban/suburban area? Want to find col-
lege-educated, white-collar workers? The bottom line here is that the
research into where to locate these people has been done, and you can
reference it for free. Once you identify who you are looking for, Pew
Research Center (PEW)[6] and other accessible sources will help.

Existing businesses simply need to examine their own clients to
determine who buys their products most. That data is a great indica-
tor that similar demographics would also be interested in becoming
a client—once they become aware of your brand. Certainly, people
can still run their own surveys and look at other marketing research if
they want more clarity, if they are entering a new market, or if they are
preparing to launch a new brand.

Seven Tips to Drive Big Results on Social Media

Want some quick tips for generating website traffic? Here are seven
proven approaches.

1. Understand the Algorithms

Every platform has an algorithm and rules that it follows to determine
who sees what. If you figure out the features noticed by the algorithm
on any given platform and adjust your strategy to maximize algorithm-
friendly posts, your chances of being seen will rise dramatically.

2. Write Catchy Posts

The general rule of thumb here is to create posts in easy-to-digest ways
that maximize a catchphrase or attention-grabbing headline. Don't
forget to break up content into sections. Use bullet points if necessary
to make sure it isn't visually intimidating. Avoiding bold fonts and
employing lower word counts work best in most cases. Use short para-
graphs and bullet points to help break up longer sections that might

---

6   Pew Research Center, https://www.pewresearch.org/.

seem visually intimidating to readers. You will likely find that content with shorter sections garners a lot more user engagement.

3. Use Hashtags

Adding popular and relevant hashtags can draw a lot more viewers to your posts. Each platform has its own hashtag preferences. Using well-followed hashtags will help you gain optimal benefit. But consider this: when you are establishing your brand identity, it may not be wise to use the most-used hashtags. Those hashtags are attached to so much content each day that your posts might get lost in the crowd. On the flip side, if you use niche hashtags, there might not be enough people searching for that content, so again, few will see it. For the best results, find hash tags with 50,000 to 1,000,000 followers.

4. Work as a Team

Encourage your employees—even incentivize them if necessary—to comment and share your company posts. The bigger the party at the time you launch your posts, the better. Most algorithms favor early responses, or what they call splash activity.

5. Pay Attention to New Trends and Features

When platforms introduce a new feature, they usually promote its use in the algorithm to encourage users to try it. If you notice a new feature, make sure you take advantage of it. The metrics of your posts will let you know when the new shine wears off. It's like getting to ride in the diamond lane as a single passenger, helping you get to your destination faster.

6. Ask Questions

Asking questions in your posts and in comments is a great way to engage people and encourage responses. Open-ended questions are the most effective. They can start a conversation that takes on a whole new life of its own.

7. Actively Comment

The number one tip I have for raising visibility on social media is to actively comment—not just on the posts you create, but in response to the posts of others. Most people will respond favorably to receiving a well-thought-out and polite comment. The more you do it, the more you will be seen and the more fans you will create.

I typically recommend spending 80% of your social media efforts commenting on the posts of others and using the other 20% to create content and respond to the comments people leave on your posts. Always respond to positive comments!

A post is a conversation starter, so don't miss the opportunity to build a relationship with those who engage with your content.

Do Not Ignore Search Engines

Did you know that at any given second, well over 99,000 searches are happening on Google alone? I've seen data to suggest there are over 8.5 billion searches on Google each day on average. Google may be the largest search engine, however, others have traction too, such as Bing, Yahoo, DuckDuckGo, and more.[7]

How can this knowledge help your business get website traffic? Your website holds information that can answer the questions search engine users are asking or help them find the product or service they are researching to purchase.

Key Concepts to Understand SEO

Search Engine Optimization—more commonly referred to as SEO—is significant. Because many people have little to no working knowledge

---

7   Maryam Mohsin, "Ten Google Search Statistics You Need to Know," Oberlo, January 13, 2023, https://www.oberlo.com/blog/google-search-statistics#:~:text=But%20how%20many%20is%20that,Internet%20Live%20Stats%2C%202022).

of how SEO works, I will define the concept, offer a strategy to understand what it means, and tell you how it works. The following definitions should help anyone grasp a more complete understanding of the advice found in the rest of this chapter. If implemented as I prescribe, the advice will help most website owners improve their SEO results.

Domain Authority

This is abbreviated as DA on most SEO tools and was introduced by the company MOZ in 2019.[8] The ranking is given to help companies understand how their website performs in search engines. On a scale from zero to 100, with 100 being "best" and zero, "worst," the average website scores somewhere between eight and 12.

Many factors help determine a website's DA score, but in my opinion, site loading speed, number of backlinks, web traffic, metadata, and keyword-rich content are the most critical. Later, I will address how to improve SEO results in detail.

Keywords

If people were trying to find the type of company you have or the services you provide, what words would they type into a search engine? The most commonly used words and phrases become your *keywords*. Keywords should appear on every page of your website and be used with high frequency in your blogs. They should also be used in alternative image descriptions and in your metadata.

Metadata

Metadata is like a wrapper on the outside of a website. It tells search engines what the website is about. Basically, it's information describing website contents—like an ingredient list. Developers fill out the information in a variety of ways, most commonly now through plugins such

---

8   Gemma Fontané, "What Domain Authority Is (and Isn't), and How to Increase It," Hubspot, June 2, 2021, https://blog.hubspot.com/marketing/domain-authority.

as Yoast. When done correctly, metadata helps a website be included as a potential "answer" match on Google or other search engines when their visitors are searching for something specific. Most technical audits I complete show that website managers have failed to fill out their metadata correctly. Make sure your website metadata is present and accurate, or Google will penalize you for it, adversely affecting your rank on their *search engine results page* (SERP).

Backlinks

A *backlink* is simply a hyperlink to another place on the internet. When clicked on, it transports the person who did the clicking to another page on the internet. There are four classifications of backlinks: *dofollow* (transport the visitor to the new location); *nofollow* (the website address does not automatically take the visitor there when clicked on); *user-generated content* (also known as UGC and normally found in the comments of blogs or social media posts); and *sponsor* (paid ads). Sponsor backlinks have two types of destinations—those on the website, referred to as *internal backlinks*; and those that lead to other websites, called *external backlinks*.

Index

Google and other search engines created indexes to help identify website content. It is important to note that websites are crawled (surveyed) and indexed at least every 30 days. The goal is to find new content and check links to ensure a page is still active. Search engines want to promote the best sources of current information. It is especially important that the information shared on a website is accurate, unique, and up to date. Beyond that, website owners want to make sure that their content matches the metadata and covers the keywords, as discussed above.

Google-Verified Business

Many people search for _____ *(fill in the blank) business near me* in search engines. The only way to be considered for these search requests by Google—the number one search engine in the world by far—is to verify your business with Google. Google offers a simple process to add your business to Google Maps and appear in general search results. When you apply, you'll receive a form to fill out by physical mail. The verification process can take anywhere from 15 to 30 days to complete, depending on the speed of the postal service.

Four Ways to Significantly Increase Search Engine Rankings

Every website should implement the following four features right away to increase search engine rankings results:

Use Video

Over 80% of internet users will eventually land on a video and hang out there for a while. Take advantage of this by ensuring each website page that you want to build website traffic on includes at least one video.

Write Longer Blog Posts

I have discovered that longer blog posts get more attention. Add at least four 1,500-word or longer blog posts per month, and make sure they include keywords about the product or service that the business wants to rank highly for in search engine queries.

Use Interactive Media

Interactive media—including videos, images, image carousels, or accordion-style information boxes (they expand by clicking on them)—are hugely advantageous for Google rankings. Why? Because in August 2022, Google Analytics moved away from cookies and updated how user engagement is tracked.

When end users scroll and click on your interactive media to validate that they are actively consuming your content, your overall Google score grows. Static images like JPEG files don't work, unless you add a link to them, so make sure to load interactive media on every page of your website that you want to perform well.

Create Pillar Content

Pillar content is new to the Google algorithm, but it is the new powder keg. Creating pillar content—blogs of 3,000 words or more that focus on your key concerns and include interactive media—will dramatically increase your SERP and overtake your competition. Your pillar content should be updated each and every month.

Avoid Overwhelm by Outsourcing if Necessary

Taking the steps outlined in this chapter will help many businesses increase their website traffic, however, the information may feel overwhelming. Building website traffic is important, but if you are not comfortable with social media or SEO—or you are simply avoiding the addition of more tasks to your workload—there are other options to think about.

Consider adding a marketing person to your team. If that is not financially realistic or a headache you don't want to endure, you can also hire a vendor. Outsource your online marketing just like many businesses do for other needs such as accounting, legal representation, information technology, human resources, and hiring recruiters. Digital marketing agencies, like the one I run at Bowman Digital Media, are available to help.[9] Finding a vendor you trust to increase website traffic for you could be the winning solution.

---

9   "Need More Sales?" Bowman Digital Media, Accessed July 6, 2023, https://bowmandigitalmedia.com/.

Evaluate and Keep on Going!

If you are not sure how effective your efforts to generate website traffic have been to date, you can check your domain authority for free. Discover where some of your website traffic is coming from using free or paid tools available on MOZ[10] or SEMrush.[11] These evaluation tools can also spot-check any website traffic and domain authority down the line, to make sure any internal or outsourced work that is being paid for is helping to improve a website's overall rankings.

Finally, future website traffic is not guaranteed based on previous efforts and as such, social media and SEO work should never stop. Please don't think of it as a sprint. Rather, consider it to be a marathon with a goal of outpacing your competition each month. The race only ends when you shut down the business.

If you implement SEO and social media efforts in a smart, effective way, you will likely be pleased with the traffic it generates. Those who put in a lot of effective effort on a consistent basis will not only build brand visibility and loyalty but also generate significantly higher and game-changing website traffic.

10   "Higher rankings. Quality traffic. Measurable results," Moz, accessed February 29, 2024, https://moz.com/.

11   "Get Measurable Results from Online Marketing," SEMrush, accessed July 6, 2023, https://www.semrush.com/.

IN THE TIME OF ARTIFICIAL INTELLIGENCE

River Jack

Writer, Digital Communicator, and Publication Director

"All of the great leaders have had one characteristic in common: it was the willingness to confront unequivocally the major anxiety of their people in their time. This, and not much else, is the essence of leadership."
— John Kenneth Galbraith, Canadian-American economist and diplomat

With **each great leap** we take as a society, we are asked to confront existential questions about ourselves. We humans tend to fear the unknown. "The unknown" often equates to "something new" and there seems to be something new—a great leap—every day. The latest unknown is artificial intelligence, better known as AI. It has been a part of our lives longer than the public realizes, operating algorithms on streaming platforms to recommend movies we might enjoy or determining the advertisements most likely to catch our attention. It is used in medical testing, banking, weather models, and so much more.

Our anxiety and excitement about AI are rooted in the untapped potential it offers. With the arrival of generative AI and its ability to create everything from artwork to scientific formulas, we are now face to face with hard questions about ownership, copyright, and human creativity. They demand complex conversations that cannot be resolved overnight but will continue for years to come.

None of us can single-handedly solve the problems created by AI or produce universal principles for using it, so I won't tell you how to incorporate AI into your business to make more money. Any guidance I could offer about the direct application of any given AI tool or software will be obsolete before I finish writing this sentence anyway!

Instead, in the spirit of *Strategic Growth,* I intend to provide you with something deeper and richer. I hope to prepare you for the onslaught of AI services, solutions, life hacks, and applications that will come knocking on the preverbal door of your business. To be a leader willing and able to confront the questions, concerns, and excitement of our time, you need curiosity, the wisdom to take one step at a time, and enthusiasm for the journey.

Beginnings

The year is 1983. Morley Safer takes one last look in the mirror to straighten his tie. A decorated journalist, having followed in the footsteps of Ernest Hemmingway as a foreign correspondent, he's made a home at CBS.[1] He's made a name for himself reporting the raw, harsh truth of the Vietnam war, earning a George Polk award, and angering President Lyndon B. Johnson—all in one fell swoop in 1965. Not shying away from a story, he's interviewed some of the most influential and powerful figures in media and government and watched the world leap forward with each technological advancement.

He has no reason to believe tonight's interview will be anything out of the ordinary. Having done his research, Morley feels confident and prepared. He walks from his dressing room to the *60 Minutes* set with an even mind.

---

1   CBS News. "'60 Minutes' Morley Safer Dies at 84." *CBS News,* https://www.cbsnews.com/news/60-minutes-morley-safer-dies-at-84/.

Cameras and production lights hum in anticipation as a steadfast, sharp-eyed woman in her 70s joins Morley in the chair across from him. Rear Admiral Grace Hopper is not just an expert, but a pioneer in the field of computers, her claim to fame being one of the first computer coders for the U.S. Navy.[2] A highly demanded lecturer and authority on computer science, Morley is eager to ask the burning questions his audience wants answers to.

The first Macintosh hasn't debuted yet, but it's coming. Computers are not just entering the workforce but the homes of everyday people.

"You talk a lot about the computer revolution. I thought we're in it, and it's over," Morley says.

"No, we're only at the beginning. We've been through the preliminaries," Grace replies.

"Well, what's it going to be like?"

Grace responds with absolute certainty: "We've got the Model T."

With all of the advanced technology around them at this moment—the cars humming down the highway, the color television sets lighting up living rooms, the workers sending electronic mail to offices across the country—it seems inconceivable to suggest this is only the beginning.

Morley wonders if Grace believes people will place too much trust in technology.

"People are scared of computers, just as I can remember, there were people who were scared to death of telephones—wouldn't go near them," she says. "There were people that thought gas light was safe but electric light wasn't very safe. We've always gone through this with every change."[3]

And change never stops.

---

2   Yale University President's Office. "Biography of Grace Murray Hopper." *Yale University President's Office*, https://president.yale.edu/biography-grace-murray-hopper.

3   CBS News. "The 60 Minutes Interview with Grace Murray Hopper." *CBS News*, https://www.cbsnews.com/news/the-60-minutes-interview-with-grace-murray-hopper/.

It is Still Brand New

We can only imagine what Rear Admiral Grace Hopper would think if she were here today. Having passed away at the age of 85 in 1992, she missed the panic of Y2K, the first iPhone, the rise of social media, and so much more. Yet, we reap the benefits of the service she and that first team of computer programmers provided back in 1944 on the Harvard IBM Mark I. Grace helped teach computers how to speak a language other than numbers.[4] Her work set in motion something inevitable: the creation of AI. We often don't stop to appreciate it all, the pioneering work that came before us.

Every industry leader, business executive, and entrepreneur should understand that all of *this*—computers, smartphones, the internet, social media, and AI—is still new. So is the *social internet* which is not shorthand for social media and the internet, but a particular era of online culture: the *creator economy*. In this economy, content creators rack up views, likes, and follows, all while growing a business.

Before we dive into a deeper conversation about AI's impact on any of this, we must discuss time. As of 2024, the social internet as we know it is roughly 15 years old. It was only in the 2010s that content creators were given viable monetization options and opportunities to grow their communities across multiple platforms, marking the age of the creator economy.

If the social internet were a person, they would just be learning to drive and still in high school, their stomach twisting in knots as a crush passes them in the hallway.

However, it can be argued that *we* are also teenagers. Teenagers, despite their unwavering sureness and because of their developing prefrontal cortex, can't comprehend what long-term consequences truly mean. Think of the last conversation you had with a teenager, trying to impart wisdom so they may learn from your experience. When you

---

4   "Grace Hopper," biography.com, accessed February 29, 2024, https://www.biography.com/scientist/grace-hopper.

said, "I was your age once," did they believe you?

Teenagers naively and firmly believe they know everything. It is not until time and maturity sink in years later that they realize they hardly knew anything at all.

It is so easy to assume we fully understand the technology we're using simply because we use it every day. Or maybe we're confident because we have the ability to crack the SEO code for ranking high in search results or know how to convert a click into a sale.

Although some of us were teenagers or full-grown adults when social media exploded into everyday life, the generation coming into the work force these days has only ever known a world with social media. The knowledge gap is already growing wider than we can jump.

Our relationship with modern technology has not matured. The truth is, the long-term consequences—good, bad, and everything in the middle—are unknown. However, this should not be cause for alarm or a call to blindly embrace changes the moment they manifest.

I can only speculate what Grace Hopper believed the future of computer technology would look like. Even if she could make incredibly informed predictions, she did not know for certain.

Neither do we.

So how do we prepare for the unknown in a rapidly evolving landscape?

An Extension of Man

I can't help but lean on the wisdom of Marshall McLuhan who is most notably recognized for his quote, "The medium is the message." It was a central idea to his body of work unpacking our ever-changing relationship with media and technology.

Reading his work now, more than two decades into the 21st Century, it feels profoundly prophetic. McLuhan explains "the medium is the message" concept most clearly the opening chapter of *Understanding Media: Extensions of Man:*

In a culture like ours, long accustomed to splitting and dividing all things as a means of control, it is sometimes a bit of a shock to be reminded that, in operational and practical fact, the medium is the message. This is merely to say that the personal and social consequences of any medium—that is, of any extension of ourselves—result from the new scale that is introduced into our affairs by each extension of ourselves, or by any new technology . . . For the "message" of any medium or technology is the change of scale or pace or pattern that it introduces into human affairs. The railway did not introduce movement or transportation or wheel or road into human society, but it accelerated and enlarged the scale of previous human functions, creating totally new kinds of cities and new kinds of work and leisure.[5]

McLuhan speaks of automation eliminating jobs as a negative result, yet we experience positive results too, such as the rise of new conveniences and entirely new industries that eventually replace the jobs lost (hopefully) and fill the time gained by it. Take migration, for example. Since the beginning of human history, we have moved from one place to another over great distances. Yet, the invention of the train, then the car, and then the airplane, did not suddenly make travel or "movement" possible. Instead, these technologies disrupted previous patterns of behavior and introduced new possibilities. They eliminated the amount of time it took to walk across the country by replacing it with flight.

Technology is a medium whose message is best understood in speed and scale. As a medium, it is bestowed real meaning by the intention behind its use. The message of the AI medium is still being shaped, but in function and form, it is a tool that operates on pattern and scale.

---

5   McLuhan, Marshall. *Understanding Media: Extensions of Man*. Signet Books, 2nd ed., January 1, 1964. pp. 23-24.

How we apply AI to our jobs, businesses, creative projects, finances, and so on is determined by how we ask it to perform our intent.

All of our tools and technological advancements are extensions of ourselves. And as information has become increasingly available to any one person with internet access, we need something to process it for us.

The conversation of ethics and AI has come into focus concerning generative AI. According to Adame Zewe in MIT News:

Generative AI can be thought of as a machine-learning model that is trained to create new data, rather than making a prediction about a specific dataset. A generative AI system is one that learns to generate more objects that look like the data it was trained on.[6]

Zewe makes the point that AI is something with which we are already familiar.

Think of the algorithms on your streaming service recommending shows and movies based on what you've already watched or an online loan calculator predicting whether or not you'll qualify for a loan based on your credit history. AI assists with social media feed recommendations, filtering what *you* are interested in out of the vast sea of online information. It operates in GPS apps, smart home devices, and online shopping recommendations. These examples of AI have gone mostly unnoticed because they don't disrupt systems; instead, they enhance our experience. The next generation of AI goes beyond predicting what we want or need; it is engineered to create something entirely new.

Tommi Jaakkola, the Thomas Siebel Professor of Electrical Engineering and Computer Science at MIT said to Adam Zewe, "We were generating things way before the last decade, but the major distinction here is in terms of the complexity of objects we can generate and the scale at which we can train these models."[7]

---

6   Adam Zewe. "Explained: Generative AI." *MIT News*, November 9, 2023, https://news.mit.edu/2023/explained-generative-ai-1109.

7   Ibid.

The ethics of generative AI is our first true taste of how this tool will test us. Appreciating the newness of this technology—and the new extensions it creates of ourselves—comes with a deeper wisdom and discernment for how to operate them. Tools such as AI can quicken our response, research, and creation time. However, if applied incorrectly, they can create more problems than they could ever solve.

Like an unlicensed teenager hell bent on driving, we want to use AI and all its capabilities *now*. So, without the developed intuition of an experienced driver, what happens when we get behind the wheel? Can we take on all the unforeseen risks and road hazards up ahead?

We have so much to learn, and there are no shortcuts without taking risks we cannot yet imagine.

No Shortcuts

Many years ago, I was coaching a client to write a memoir. Incredibly confident in her speaking skills, she would address chosen topics for more than an hour at a time with little to no preparation. But when it came to sitting down and drafting her story, she struggled to find momentum.

I suggested she dictate her story instead of writing it. She followed my instructions to record a voice memo on her daily walks, and later after returning home, manually transcribe it.

The experiment was a success. Within a handful of walk-recording sessions, she found her writing stride. Manual transcription helped her translate one confidence skill into another. It wasn't long after this strategy was implemented that she grew secure enough in her writing skills that she abandoned recording voice memos. Of her own accord, my client found herself less avoidant of revising her words and leaning into the writing process.

Later that year, another client with a similar background—confident and radiant in her public speaking skills but struggling to sit and speak through the keyboard—came to me for help. I gave her the same instructions.

Although she was thrilled with the idea, she took a shortcut. She acquired transcription software to type as she spoke. (Keep in mind, this was at a time before voice-to-text software was not as accessible or robust as it is today.) I did my best to encourage her to go through her voice recordings, but she wouldn't budge. This shortcut cost her the opportunity to strengthen her writing confidence skills and created more tedious work in the editing process.

In some ways, it's unfair to compare the amount of time it took each client to finish their manuscripts. My philosophy has always been to let the process take the time it *needs*. With that said, client number two struggled longer to find her footing as she clung to an unproductive sense of urgency.

This mildly cautionary tale illustrates how a tool's use is influenced by the intention behind it. McLuhan recognized long ago that technology speeds up processes, but also it does not eliminate all obstacles or friction. What may seem like a short-term calculated risk can lead to unknown consequences in the future. If anything, new tools solve old problems while creating new ones. Long-term success is a product of discernment.

Adapt and Adopt

It's a clear, cool winter Wednesday in Atlanta, and a man sits at his desk with sunlight cascading from the skylights above. It's the perfect architecture for his home office, with an abundance of natural light to take advantage of during his video calls.

He sends out the invite link for a meeting and waits for his guest to join. A friend and creative collaborator wants to pick his brain about AI and the unavoidable changes further adoption of the technology will bring.

In my home office, I get a ping to join a meeting. I take one last look in my monitor's camera before clicking the link and greeting my friend Dale Adams, Founder and CEO of an AI consulting studio,

Atelier Post-Architekts. I have had the opportunity to work with Dale on his creative projects, and he keeps me up to date with generative AI advancements. Because of Dale, I'm aware of how these publicly available AI tools enhance creative production.

As our conversation begins, Dale turns on an AI assistant that will summarize our on-camera conversation rather than recording our meetings which would leave us with hours of playback to scrub through. (The summary I received later was impressively organized and thorough, providing an efficient reference for writing this chapter.)

Dale understands better than anyone I've met how the AI revolution compares to the computer revolution of the recent past. So, I had to ask him where he sees AI fitting into business now and in the rapidly approaching future.

"As with previous technological revolutions, individuals are going to need to level up their skills to use these new AI tools. Except the timeframe is going be at hyper speed over the next three to five years versus 15 years for the computer revolution," Dale says.

Of course, AI is expected to revolutionize the workforce. From Dale's perspective, it only makes sense to make a move toward generalized knowledge in the workplace. Similar to the shift brought on by widespread adoption of computers and the internet in the late '80s and early '90s, there is a learning curve with AI.

It should come as no surprise that companies will increasingly expect their employees to be proficient in using AI tools. Those who fail to keep up may not be hired in the future. The required skillset shift applies not just to employees, but leaders at the top. C-Suite executives and business leaders need to stay on their toes as well. If business and industry leaders fail to understand the tools and applications running their enterprises, the knowledge gap will grow, undermining employee education and development.

But there are greater consequences to consider. Dale forecasts job displacement for senior personnel who do not learn these new tools.

"With a recent 2024 report from the IMF (the International Monetary Fund), AI will have a larger impact on high-skilled workers in four years. I believe companies will need to invest heavily into AI to upskill current employees' knowledge as the wage gap widens on workers who have AI skills with those who don't. So, onboarding employee AI education program will become necessary or older employees like Gen X will be lost in the marketplace without the necessary skills," Dale says.

Knowledge gaps must be filled, excuses denied. Failing to understand how to turn a Word document into a PDF is a small, frustrating quirk of feigned computer incompetence that should not be overlooked. Nor should any leader tolerate self-inflicted ignorance in AI applications.

According to an International Monetary Fund (IMF) blog from mid-January 2024 it was reported that "younger workers may find it easier to exploit opportunities while older workers could struggle to adapt."[8]

Companies will need to continue investing in their employees to maintain productivity and prevent costly turnover. An employee who goes unheard in conversations about incorporating AI for product development and customer service will seek out a leader who gives them a seat at the table.

As a leader, you'll need to be well-versed enough to identify and address these challenges, or at the very least, understand enough to outsource expertise in AI application. So, let's take a closer look at how this might actually work.

---

8   Georgieva, Kristalina. "AI Will Transform the Global Economy: Let's Make Sure It Benefits Humanity." *IMF Blogs*, International Monetary Fund, https://www.imf.org/en/Blogs/Articles/2024/01/14/ai-will-transform-the-global-economy-lets-make-sure-it-benefits-humanity.

For Your Consideration

Let's say you have an employee who's tasked with taking notes during meetings. Like Dale, you decide to use an AI assistant instead. Now that you have an unpaid, low-cost assistant to take those notes, what happens to your employee?

You could fire them and save a few bucks, but there is an alternative. With the mundane but important task of note-taking eliminated, consider adding a new and greater responsibility to fill the time for the assistant. Can their current skillset be used in another area, or can you invest in developing other skills?

Do not rush the adoption and adaptation process or you might end up eliminating the most valuable asset to your enterprise: the people you are leading toward a united goal. Instead, consider the following three guideposts for embracing AI and using it to your advantage.

1. Take One Step at a Time

Yes, technology is advancing at faster and faster rates, but you need not try to keep up for posterity's sake. While these advancements may seem challenging or even overwhelming, remember, you're not an impulsive teenager. You are a leader who takes no shortcuts, and you understand long-lasting progress is made one step at a time. So, with each new AI tool made available to you and your company, ask yourself:

- Will this eliminate a task or role in my company?

- What is the negative result of that and how can I ensure there is a greater positive result as well?

- Is this particular tool worth taking our time to understand and utilize?

2. Stay Curious

The advice to stay curious as a leader goes beyond the topic of artificial intelligence, but it certainly applies well here. Keep an open mind. You have the capacity to learn, grow, and confront any anxieties provoked by AI integration. Ask yourself:

- Will this AI tool improve productivity for my business and my employees?
- What do my partners and employees have to say about this? Can their input help me determine the best path forward?
- How can I ensure using this tool will not negatively affect the integrity of my business and my people?

3. Embrace the Journey

We can look to experts and theorists for predictions of what to expect with each technological advancement, including widespread use of AI. Yet, the unknown is just that—unknown. As a society, we must confront the challenges that come with AI. As a leader, you should not shy away from such a challenge. Here are some final questions for you to consider:

- Do I have enough knowledge about these tools to make an informed decision about using AI in my industry?
- Is my business ready to embrace the changes AI will bring to my industry?
- If not, what can I do to help us be ready?

Your company may pride itself with AI-free products and services, or it may innovate with AI assistance. Either path offers its own anxieties, but whichever path you choose—or how many times you change course as you learn new information—embracing the journey with your team, your colleagues, and your partners will ensure every strategic step toward growth bears fruit.

BIOGRAPHIES

Kelly E. Babcock

Kelly Babcock lives in the Columbus, Ohio area where she is a labor and employment lawyer representing Ohio public sector clients in various HR matters. She recently transitioned to a full-time training director role for the statewide firm and sits on the board of directors. Kelly is passionate about helping people overcome stress, burnout, and other mental health and addiction issues with natural, holistic practices. As a result of her research and personal journey, Kelly became a licensed hemp (CBD/CBG) cultivator in 2020 in Ohio.

Ira Bowman

With six-figure follower counts each on LinkedIn and Instagram, and a five-figure following on YouTube, Ira Bowman knows the online digital world. Since June 2020, with the launch of his business, Bowman Digital Media, Ira focuses on increasing visibility for his clients on social media and increasing their website traffic. He holds a bachelor's degree from Liberty University. Ira currently lives in Southern California, just outside Los Angeles with his wife of 20-plus years and their eight children.

Carol Carpenter

Carol is an entrepreneur, TEDx speaker, author, stuntwoman, actress, and mother of two adult boys. Her unconventional upbringing has given her a unique insight into how she views the world. A first-generation female born in the United States to immigrant parents from Taiwan, Carol grew up experiencing contrasts: two cultures, (American and Taiwanese), two languages (English and Taiwanese), and two religions (Presbyterian and Buddhist). It is with this perspective she's built successful businesses: Carol is the Founder of MotoVixens, Managing Partner of Iron Dog Media, and co-host of the *Titan Evolution Podcast*. She has a signature line of products, a reality show, and is executive producer of an upcoming movie, *The Strange*.

Cynthia Davis

During a career spanning more than 30 years, Cynthia Davis reached the highest echelons of leadership in highly respected organizations including General Electric, Lockheed Martin, Raytheon, and Bausch & Lomb. She co-created one of the most unconventional and successful consulting, training, and business advisory firms, Radiant Blue, LLC. As a highly sought-after executive advisor, Cynthia's work with entrepreneurs and business leaders navigates the challenges of business growth, personal and business transitions, cultural change and transformation, and readying their teams for mission success.

Tom Finn

Tom Finn is the Co-Founder of LeggUP, a professional development organization and host of *The Talent Empowerment Podcast*. He offers committed, capable, bold leadership that inspires and uplifts the global community. Dedicated to helping leaders figure out how to deliver productivity and well-being in the workplace, he has a mission to improve the culture of organizations, which ultimately improves the global community.

Deborah Froese

Deborah Froese is on a mission: to spark change through the power of story. An award-winning fiction author with a broad portfolio of published nonfiction to her credit, Deborah has been working for more than 20 years as an editor and story coach with writers who share her passion. The *For Leaders* series is a particular delight; she views it as an extended series of tools and inspiration for changing the world through business.

Dan Grech

Dan Grech is the founder and CEO of BizHack Academy, whose mission is to give small business owners a simpler way to grow. Dan is a Pulitzer Prize-winning former NPR and PBS journalist turned entrepreneur and educator, and he carries forward a family legacy of teaching and coaching. Past career highlights include serving as the head of marketing at two software startups and the nation's largest Hispanic-owned energy company; working as a correspondent for NPR's *Marketplace*, PBS's *Nightly Business Report*, and *The Miami Herald*; and being an instructor at Princeton, Columbia, and the University of Miami. Dan is a graduate of Princeton University, has two master's degrees, and was a Fulbright scholar. He lives in Miami with his wife, Gretchen Beesing, and two children.

River Jack

River Jack (aka River Chau) is a writer and talker of internet things, social media culture, and being a creator in digital times. Her background in creative writing, digital communication, film and video production, and publishing drives her passions. River is an advocate for creatives carving their own path and finding their authentic voice. She brings her aptitude for storytelling and navigating the digital age to her role as the Publication Director at Indigo River Publishing in an ever-evolving industry.

Liz Lathan

Over a career spanning more than 20 years, Liz Lathan, certified meeting professional (CMP), has shared her skills through stints at multiple Fortune 50 companies. She is the founder of several companies in the event space and currently runs The Community Factory with with her business partner, Nicole Osibodu. Together, they are revolutionizing the way participants engage at events through their Spontaneous Think Tank format for peer-to-peer engagement. Liz also runs their two proprietary communities, Club Ichi for B2B event marketers and Team CMO for heads of marketing.

Megan McInnis

Megan McInnis has worked with small, medium, and large nonprofits for over 20 years. She founded Doing Good, the 501c3 nonprofit which provides agencies marketing and public relations tools and opportunities to share their volunteer stories. This B2B nonprofit serves nationwide and is 100% remote. Doing Good celebrates those who do good! McInnis also teaches nonprofit management graduate courses and was awarded The President's Volunteer Service Award for the United States of America. Plus, she owns The Consultancy which serves those who serve others. She proudly lives in The Volunteer State of Tennessee.

Nicole Osibodu

Nicole Osibodu loves to play the game, "You know what would be really fun?" For the past 20-plus years, Nicole has used this question and parlayed her intuitive talent to engage and inspire people into building relationships that transcend business. With her business partner, Liz Lathan, she created a company based on creating these connections. The Community Factory is her shining example of how strangers become friends and how friends become family—and it proves that profitable relationships benefit everyone.

David Peters

David Peters is the Founder and Owner of Peters Professional Education (petersprofessionaleducation.com) and Peters Tax Preparation & Consulting, PC. He is also a financial advisor for CFO Capital Management. He has over 15 years of experience in financial services, including three years in the hedge fund industry and six years in the insurance industry. In addition to running his own professional education website, David regularly teaches courses in accounting, finance, insurance, financial planning, and ethics throughout the United States.

Dan Vega

Dan Vega started his first business at 19 and has been writing and speaking in the field of business ever since. He has achieved success in several careers including sales, marketing, management, corporate restructuring, and consulting.

Dan is one of the top experts in the country assisting companies secure funding. He now holds ownership in several successful companies and is personally invested in several spaces in the market including film and television, technology, health, environmental, spirits, art, and fashion.